WAKE

THE STORY OF A BATTLE

WAKE
The Story of a Battle

by IRVING WERSTEIN

MAPS BY AVA MORGAN

THOMAS Y. CROWELL COMPANY
NEW YORK

BY THE AUTHOR

THE BATTLE OF MIDWAY

THE BATTLE OF AACHEN

GUADALCANAL

WAKE *The Story of a Battle*

Designed by Ava Morgan

*Manufactured in the United States of America
by the Vail-Ballou Press, Inc., Binghamton, New York*

Library of Congress Catalog Card No. 64-20693

FIRST PRINTING

This book is dedicated to
Captain Bill Reid, his wife, Nan, and
their three sons: Mitchell, Martin, and Nigel.

Author's Note

THIS BOOK DEALS with a battle fought far out in the Central Pacific at the very outset of American participation in World War II. The battle was for possession of an obscure place called Wake Atoll. An accident of geography gave it military and strategic importance, and young men were killed fighting there in December, 1941.

A gallant band of American Marines, swashbuckling Leathernecks, lived up to the traditions of the Corps by defending Wake for 15 days against insuperable odds.

They fought alone, without help or reinforcement. In that fateful December, when the Japanese struck at Pearl Harbor to destroy the battleships of the United States Pacific Fleet, confusion and ineptness crippled the United States Navy more than had the Japanese bombs.

Only a handful of American fighting men were prepared to face the wily enemy. The United States Marines on Wake were in the forefront. There was nothing extraordinary about the garrison there; some were youths who had joined the Marine Corps for adventure; others were veteran Leathernecks with service in many places around the world.

They were not knights in shining armor but brash men ready for anything; they came from farms and cities; some had little education, others were college and university graduates. They were grocery clerks, mechanics, bank tellers, truck drivers, teachers, long-shoremen, and teen-agers who had never held a steady job. These men of divergent backgrounds had a common bond: their pride in being Marines.

Perhaps, to outsiders, that pride seemed overween-ing. But on Wake—and in the many terrible battles that followed during the Pacific War—the Marines lived up to the prowess with which they had so boast-fully endowed themselves.

This is a re-creation of the 15-day-long drama en-acted on Wake Atoll from December 8 to 23, 1941. I had no intention of making war glorious or glamorous. It was my purpose to tell the story of a battle and the men who fought it. I have tried to portray the Japanese ac-curately, and not to malign or caricature them.

For a book such as this one, I have not included many of the complex and intricate details that make up the jigsaw pieces of a battle. Aside from that, every-thing was as I have recorded it in that predoomed struggle of the Marines.

What happened at Wake, coming on the heels of

Pearl Harbor, shocked the American people. Not since the Civil War had the nation come so close to total disaster. Fortunately, Americans have the quality of getting up off the floor with both fists swinging—as the enemy learned during almost four years of unrelenting warfare.

In preparing this book I had advice and guidance from many people. Among them were: Lieutenant Colonel Herbert Baine, Marine Corps Public Information Office, New York City; Dr. James J. Heslin and the staff of the New-York Historical Society Library; J. J. Tarrant, Lieutenant USNR (Ret.); Leon Weidman, New York Public Library; the staff of the New York Newspaper Library; Commander D. D. Overby, Office of Information, Department of the Navy; and John Augustin, United States Information Agency. Miss Clemence Haefelfinger and Miss Althea Lister of Pan American Airways provided interesting material about the Philippine Clipper on Wake Island.

I must also thank my agent, Miss Candida Donadio, for helping smooth out many rough spots. My wife was a stanch ally, always ready with a sympathetic ear. My young son waited until after working hours before enticing me into fun and games. Mrs. Lee Levin, who typed the manuscript, deserves special thanks for her promptness and efficiency.

I. W.

Contents

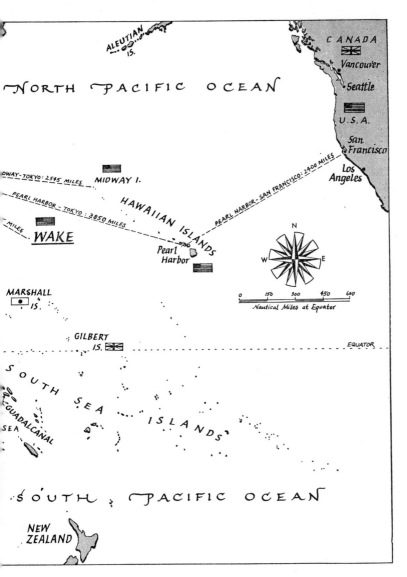

MAP OF THE PACIFIC AND FAR EAST BEFORE DECEMBER 7, 1941.

1. *"Soon the glorious hour..."*

ADMIRAL ISOROKU YAMAMOTO, the fifty-seven-year-old Commander-in-Chief, Combined Fleet, Imperial Japanese Navy, frowned at a map of the Central Pacific Area, spread out on a large table in a conference room of his Tokyo Headquarters. Next to him stood stocky fifty-two-year-old Vice Admiral Nariyoshi Inouye, Commander, Fourth Fleet, Imperial Japanese Navy, based at Truk in the Caroline Islands.

Bespectacled, shaven-headed Inouye could scarcely conceal his satisfaction at this meeting with Yamamoto. It meant the Fourth Fleet chief had not been overlooked by the High Command. Even though he held flag rank,

1

Inouye felt his present assignment to be an inferior one. The bobtail assortment of old cruisers, aging destroyers, venerable submarines, and obsolescent land-based aircraft of the Fourth Fleet made it far from the Imperial Navy's prize command.

But any discontent that Inouye had harbored disappeared that bleak morning in November, 1941, as he squinted at the spot on the map indicated by Admiral Yamamoto. The Imperial Navy's commander pointed to American-held Wake Atoll, which consisted of three islands—Wake, Peale, and Wilkes—far out in the Central Pacific, some 1,000 miles west of U. S.-owned Midway Island and 1,300 miles east of American Guam. Tiny Wake stretched only 13,500 yards from its northern to its southern tip. But this blob of volcanic land rising out of the ocean was an important link in a projected chain of U. S. naval and air bases meant to girdle the Central Pacific. Should war break out between the United States and Japan, Wake's role would become vital. It outflanked major Japanese bases in the Marshall and Gilbert islands.

In 1941, lonely Wake Atoll was receiving unprecedented attention from Japanese militarists, for war clouds had gathered over the Pacific. Japan's aggressive policies were making a showdown with the United States bound to come sooner or later.

A Japanese-American war had been made inevitable

when militant Imperial Army and Navy chiefs revived an ancient Japanese credo known as *Hakko Ichiu*—roughly translated as "bringing the eight corners of the world under one roof"—or Japan's domination of Asia and the Pacific. Some Japanese nationalists went further and dreamed of global rule by Nippon.

After being dormant for centuries, *Hakko Ichiu* was reborn in 1921; that year a Japanese fascist named Ikki Kita wrote a book that was the blueprint for a "New Era" in Japan. Kita's ideology, known as *Kodo-Ha*, presented an Oriental version of Hitlerism.

Among other things, he proposed a regime that would practice suppression of political criticism, abolish representative government, and carry out territorial expansion for Japan. *Kodo-Ha* gained a wide following among Army officers when Kita called for "freeing" 700 million Japanese "blood brothers" in India, China, the Philippines, and European Asiatic colonies where "the white devils are grinding our kinsmen into the dust."

Kodo-Ha fanatics rose to political power in Japan by eliminating the opposition through terror and assassinations. Once *Kodo-Ha* supporters held high office, Japan embarked on a series of military adventures. The first was launched in September, 1931, when the Imperial Army marched into Manchuria on a trumped-up excuse.

The Mikado's soldiers soon conquered all Manchuria, which they renamed Manchukuo, "Dove of Peace"—for the men who had led the unprovoked invasion saw themselves as peacemakers. To them, peace was Japanese control of the Orient—a rule gained by "righteous force"—should Nippon's Oriental "blood brothers" need to be convinced of the advantages awaiting them under the "benevolent protection" of the Emperor Hirohito.

The next rung on Japan's "ladder to peace" was the invasion of northern China in 1933. This started a long and bitter struggle filled with dangerous international incidents, one of which brought Japan and the United States to the brink of war. In December, 1937, Japanese planes deliberately bombed and sank an American gunboat, the USS *Panay*, on the Yangtze River. It took skillful diplomacy, profound Nipponese apologies, and steep reparations to preserve a tenuous peace in the Pacific for a few more years.

By 1941, despite Chinese resistance, Japan controlled most of China's coastal areas and such important cities as Nanking and Shanghai. World War II, then entering its third year, had not yet spread to the Pacific, but threatened to do so at any moment. Sorely in need of oil and other materials for a full-scale war, Japan was tempted to spread southward and seize Sumatra, Malaya, the Netherlands East Indies, the Philippines, Borneo, Burma, Thailand, Indochina, Australia, New Zealand, and the South Seas islands, with all the vast natural resources of the Pacific.

Back in 1937, Japan had signed a pact with Germany and Italy in which she pledged to help Adolf Hitler and Benito Mussolini annihilate so-called decadent democracies and "exterminate" communism. The prime targets of the Rome-Berlin-Tokyo Axis were the United States, Great Britain, and Soviet Russia. Ironically, for the purposes of the pact, Hitler declared the Japanese "racially pure" and deemed them "honorary Aryans," although he had once classified the yellow race as "mongrels."

Shortly after signing the pact with the Nazis and the Fascists, the Japanese attempted a perilous venture: an invasion of Soviet Siberia from Manchukuo. The Russians met the Imperial Army at the border and trounced the Mikado's warriors in a series of pitched battles.

After this setback, Japan was wary of clashing with Russia again. She turned down a suggestion made by Hitler early in 1941 to declare war against the Soviet Union. The Führer's request puzzled the Japanese. Why had the Germans asked them to fight the Russians when Hitler himself had signed a nonaggression pact with them?

That mystery was cleared up by mid-1941. In June, Hitler astounded the world by springing a savage surprise attack on Russia. This created a paradoxical situation, which saw the Russian dictator, Josef Stalin, become an ally of England, whose Prime Minister, Winston Churchill, was one of Soviet Russia's archcritics.

A cartoon of the day depicted Stalin and Churchill

singing the chorus of a popular song: "You made me love you; I didn't want to do it . . ."

As that fateful year rolled on, Hitler's armies fought in the arctic cold of approaching Russian winter; and the lesser Axis partner, Italy's Duce, Benito Mussolini, sent his Blackshirt Legions across the hot sands of North Africa toward the Suez Canal. An early total victory for the Axis partners seemed imminent. No man could foretell that Hitler's Wehrmacht (Army) was slated to meet disaster in Russia or that Mussolini's grandiose dreams would end ignominiously.

The jealous Japanese saw only immediate triumphs for Mussolini and Hitler, not future catastrophe. The *Kodo-Ha* men seethed because the world was being "pulled together" under the Italo-German roof; Occidentals, not Orientals, were achieving *Hakko Ichiu*. This proved too unpalatable for the *Kodo-Ha* fanatics, whose leader was the Premier of Japan, General Hideki Tojo. Something had to be done very soon to make Japanese supremacy in Asia and the Pacific an accomplished fact before Hitler's shadow fell across the Pacific as it had over the Atlantic. Tojo began making plans without consulting his Axis cohorts. The Pacific was to be a Japanese preserve, barred to all poachers—including Germany and Italy.

The prime deterrent to Tojo's ambitions in the Pacific was the U. S. Navy, which was big and powerful although the Imperial Supreme War Council regarded it with disdain. In fact, Japan's warmongers were scornful of everything American. They derided the "despicable" U. S. Army and the "ridiculous" U. S. Navy and scoffed at the American people.

"The mercenary Yankee has no stomach for war. . . . He cares only for soft living, luxuries and money. . . . In all America there exists not a man, woman or child who knows the meaning of patriotism or sacrifice for country," wrote a Japanese journalist in 1941.

Convinced that the United States could be speedily defeated, Tojo and his followers asked Emperor Hirohito to give his blessings for war against America. While the Mikado did not overtly consent to the war on America, neither did he forbid it. The "Son of Heaven" kept a discreet silence as his generals and admirals plotted how best to crush the Yankees.

Somehow, the results of their discussions leaked out, and early in 1941 the U. S. Ambassador to Japan, Mr. Joseph C. Grew, made a diary entry: "There is a lot of talk around Tokyo to the effect that the Japanese, in case of war with America, are planning to go all out in a surprise mass air attack at Pearl Harbor. . . . Of course, I informed our government."

(Mr. Grew's prophetic and accurate information was disregarded by U. S. Naval Intelligence. "We place absolutely no credence in such an absurd rumor," Chief of Naval Operations [CNO] Admiral Harold R. Stark wrote Admiral Husband E. Kimmel, Commander-in-Chief, Pacific Fleet [CINCPAC], with headquarters at Pearl Harbor.)

Time ran swiftly in 1941. The Imperial Supreme War Council completed its master plan for the Pacific War— a bold scheme of conquest with four main points:

1. Simultaneous landings of amphibious forces in Luzon, Guam, the Malay Peninsula, and Hong Kong. All to be preceded by air attacks.

2. Carrier air attack on the U. S. Pacific Fleet at Pearl Harbor.

3. Rapid exploitation of initial successes by the seizure of Manila, Mindanao, Wake Atoll, the Bismarcks, Bangkok, and Singapore.

4. Occupation of the Dutch East Indies and continuation of the war with China.

(The Japanese intended to enlarge the scope of the war by embroiling Great Britain and the Netherlands as well as the United States.)

The Imperial Supreme War Council did not unanimously support this project. The chief objector was Admiral Yamamoto, one of the Council's most influential members. He vainly pointed out the tremendous industrial potential of the United States and its huge reserve of manpower. If Japan were to be victorious in such a conflict, he warned, the victory had to be won swiftly.

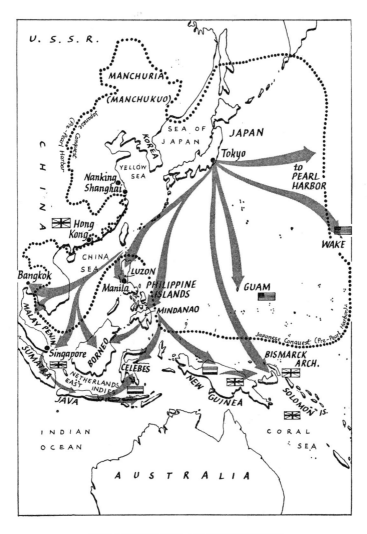

THE JAPANESE PLAN OF CONQUEST

In a drawn-out struggle, the odds were all with the Americans.

"If I am told to fight regardless of consequence, I shall run wild . . . for the first six months or a year . . . but I can make no predictions . . . I have no confidence for the second and third years . . . of such a war," Yamamoto reputedly told a former high Japanese cabinet minister.

Despite Yamamoto's opposition, the Council approved the four-point war plan, which was to be launched during the first week in December, 1941. The exact date was left open and designated as X-Day.

Although displeased by the Council's decision, Admiral Yamamoto, an officer who knew how to take as well as give orders, energetically prepared for X-Day. By late November he sent for individual fleet commanders to brief them on their X-Day roles. Vice Admiral Chuichi Nagumo was awarded the plum: command of the First Air Fleet, the carrier force attacking Pearl Harbor. Second billing came to Vice Admiral Inouye.

Yamamoto personally gave the Fourth Fleet chief his orders: "On X-Day, you will seize Guam and attack Wake Atoll by air. When Wake's planes and defense guns have been knocked out, you will despatch an amphibious force to capture it and establish an air and sea base on the Atoll."

Inouye permitted himself a slight smile. He bowed

stiffly. "I thank the Emperor and you for putting so much trust and confidence in me. I shall not fail."

"That is why you were chosen for this mission, Admiral. Do you have any questions?" Yamamoto asked.

"Only one, sir. When is X-Day?"

"That you will learn in good time. Soon the glorious hour will come. Very soon," Yamamoto said and grinned at Inouye.

2. *"I'm so happy you're in the Pacific"*

NOBODY HAD PAID much notice to Wake Atoll for several centuries after its accidental discovery in 1568 by the Spanish explorer Alvaro de Mendaña who, while roaming the Pacific, put in there with two ships for fresh water and food.

Mendaña found neither water nor food and left at once after noting that ". . . the land swarms with a strange type of rat that runs about on its hind legs . . . and there are many birds of all sorts."

He named the unprepossessing place San Francisco, but failed to note it on his charts. Mendaña's find was soon lost in oblivion, and remained so for more than 200 years. In 1796, a British merchantman, the *Prince William Henry,* touched at the atoll. The ship's skipper, Captain William Wake, went ashore for a closer look at the islands he had sighted from afar.

Immodestly naming the atoll and its largest island for himself, Captain Wake hauled anchor and departed. He added the atoll to his map, showing it as a V-shaped mass made up of three separate islands, each covered with dense, low brush and surrounded by coral reefs that ran at a distance varying from 30 to 1,100 yards offshore.

Capt. Wake wrote: ". . . the sea roars continually on the white sand beaches . . . the surf is loud, booming like a hundred cannon. . . . The only entry to the lagoon is a fifty-yard wide gap between two islands. . . . The lagoon is studded with coral heads that can rip the bottom out of a boat."

Wake lay forgotten until December 20, 1840, when Commodore Charles Wilkes, U. S. Navy, on an oceanographic expedition in the Pacific, surveyed and mapped the atoll. In his party was Titian Peale, a government naturalist, who explored the land area and the waters around Wake. One of the smaller islands was named in his honor. The third island became known as Wilkes, for the expedition's commander.

Nearly 60 years passed before the United States took formal possession of the three islands. On January 17,

1899, Commander E. D. Taussig arrived off Wake aboard the gunboat USS *Bennington*. He sent a boat ashore, raised and lowered an American flag, fired a salute, and proclaimed it to be United States territory.

The decades marched by and Wake slumbered. No human lived there. The surf pounding on the coral reef was heard only by the innumerable birds whose cries and screeches echoed across the boundless waters.

Wake remained a sanctuary for teal, frigate birds, bosun birds, gooneys, and a species known as the flightless rail. The only other living creatures there were the rats, which swarmed by the thousands through the thick underbrush.

Occasionally, a ship sent a boat to inspect the isolated islands. Once in a while, Japanese fishermen cast their nets near Wake; from time to time, hunters would drop off to shoot birds and collect feathers. But on the whole, it was unchanged by the passing years.

Then, time and progress caught up with Wake. After World War I, the airplane came of military and commercial age. Naval aircraft carriers, once regarded as impractical gadgets by mossback admirals and Navy Department bureaucrats, became vital parts of the U. S. Fleet. Carrier-borne bombing, torpedo and fighter planes were developed. Tactics were created to use such aircraft as offensive weapons. The rise of naval air power sounded the death knell of traditional navies.

The U. S. Navy began an anxious search for air bases in the Pacific during the early 1930's as Japanese aggressions mounted. Wake Atoll suddenly assumed strategic value. It was an ideal "fixed aircraft carrier" according to one high-ranking naval officer. Considerable interest arose in converting that remote outpost into an advanced base for naval patrol planes and bombers. "Properly fortified, Wake will be a dagger at Japan's throat in case of war," one admiral declared. But an economy-minded Congress paid little heed to the Navy's demands, which also included appropriations for putting an air base on distant Guam.

But as Congress shuffled papers and took no action about either Wake or Guam, Pan American Airways decided, in 1935, to inaugurate a transpacific service using huge Martin-130 (Clipper) seaplanes. The proposed route was to run between San Francisco and Manila, with overnight stops at Honolulu, Midway, Wake, and Guam. Capable of carrying thirty passengers plus a five-man crew, the Clippers were to begin weekly San Francisco–Manila flights in November, 1936.

A Pan American construction crew went to Wake in the spring of 1935 and built a weather station, radio transmitter, hotel, and seaplane ramp on the southern shore of Peale Island, where the lagoon was suitable for landing the Clippers.

Once the flights started, Wake no longer slumbered

in the sun, rain, and sea. Twice every week the big planes arrived for refueling and an overnight stay. The Pan American station personnel set out a vegetable garden and a catchment for rainwater. Human beings now shared Wake with the birds and the rats.

Once the Clippers began to use Wake, the Navy renewed its clamor for an advanced air base there. In 1938, Rear Admiral A. J. Hepburn, USN, conducted an investigation as to the suitability of this proposal. His report recommended a 7.5-million-dollar, 3-year development program for the atoll with proper naval installations on Peale, Wilkes, and Wake islands. (In his report, Wake meant the entire atoll and included all three islands. Individual islands were separately named.)

Hepburn suggested building facilities for submarines as well. He also felt that Guam should be similarly improved. Although his report had been issued in 1938, it took 2 years for Congress to move. And not until 1940 were funds appropriated—not 7.5 million dollars but 20 million dollars for the construction on Wake. However, Congress refused to allot any money for Guam.

"We can't toss public funds around like confetti. People know about Wake because the Clippers land there, but who ever heard of Guam?" a Midwestern Congressman said. "Anyway, we can't make the Japanese mad by building a base on Guam, right in their front yard . . ."

During 1940, Contractors Pacific Naval Bases, Inc., a civilian company, was awarded the contract for building installations on Wake. By January, 1941, some 1,100 civilian workers were unloading bulldozers, road scrapers, and digging and dredging equipment.

A crude camp (Camp No. 1) was built on Wake Island's southern coast to house the civilians. (Later, Camp No. 2, a more elaborate affair, was erected on the northern tip of Wake Island; it included a post exchange, a well-equipped hospital, comfortable barracks, and a movie theater.)

Before long, the civilians under a dynamic engineer, Nathan Dan Teters, had bulldozed an airstrip near Peacock Point on Wake Island. Thirty-foot-wide coral-topped roads were cut through. The channel between Wake and Wilkes islands was dredged and the lagoon cleared of coral heads. Work also started on steel, glass, and concrete buildings. On Peale Island a naval hospital, marine barracks, transmitter, seaplane ramps, and control towers were started. Over on Wilkes Island, the only construction then contemplated was a number of permanent fuel storage tanks.

All this American activity aroused Japanese curiosity. At intervals, Imperial Navy observation planes appeared over Wake, leisurely flying back and forth snapping aerial photographs; the type and extent of Yankee preparations were no secret to the Japanese High Command.

On April 18, 1941, barely 2 months after he had been appointed CINCPAC, Admiral Kimmel wrote to Admiral Stark, CNO, from Pearl Harbor. Kimmel stressed Wake's key position in the event of war in the Pacific. Urging that the atoll be strongly defended with troops, guns and planes, he stated:

". . . to recapture Wake if the Japanese should seize it in the early period of hostilities would require operations of some magnitude. Since the Japanese 4th Fleet includes transports and troops . . . suited for landing operations, it appears not unlikely that one of the initial operations of the Japanese may be directed against Wake . . ."

Kimmel concluded by requesting that substantial units of the 1st Defense Battalion, U. S. Marines, then at Pearl Harbor, be sent to Wake not later than June 1, 1941.

The defense battalion was a new development in the Marine Corps, conceived in 1939, for holding and securing an atoll such as Wake. At full strength it consisted of 43 officers and 909 men to man three 5-inch semi-mobile coastal batteries each with two guns; four 3-inch antiaircraft (AA) batteries of four guns apiece with range finders, computers, and fire-control directors; a radar and searchlight unit; forty-eight .50-caliber machine guns for antiaircraft; and forty-eight .30-caliber machine guns for beach defense. Individual Marines were armed with '03 Springfield rifles; they wore light khaki uniforms and World War I type steel helmets and had sidearms and hand grenades.

In the light of growing tensions between the United States and Japan, even the hidebound Navy Department could not ignore Kimmel's prophetic warning. It took time for the Navy's ponderous administrative machinery to get into motion, and it was not until August 1 that 6 officers and 173 enlisted men of the 1st Marine Defense Battalion tramped aboard the transport USS *Regulus* at Pearl Harbor. They landed at Wake on August 19 after an uneventful voyage, and started to dig gun emplacements under the direction of Major Lewis A. Holm, who commanded this advance detail.

On October 15, Major James P. Devereux arrived with the battalion's weapons, equipment, and more Marines. Due to circumstances there was a dearth of men and weapons. Only one 3-inch AA battery had complete fire-control equipment.

The radar was lacking and Devereux brought only twenty-four .50-caliber AA machine guns, not the anticipated forty-eight. Even when another batch of Marines arrived on November 2, the garrison's Marine personnel numbered about 400 enlisted men and officers. This was a prime example of "too little, too late," the malady then infecting the democracies. On Wake, there were all kinds of shortages. The Marines needed more food, weapons, and ammunition in case of a drawn-out siege.

Upon his arrival in October, Major Devereux relieved Holm as Marine Commanding Officer (CO). A slight, active man of about forty, with many years in the Marine Corps, Devereux set up a command post (CP) near Peacock Point on Wake Island and rushed defensive preparations. In addition to that duty, Devereux was also CO of the atoll except for the civilian workers, who did not come under military control.

The Marines worked around the clock from the time they set foot on Wake. Besides placing the 5-inch and 3-inch batteries at strategic points on Wake, Peale, and Wilkes islands, putting in communication lines and stringing wire for field telephones, they also had to unload supply ships, dig entrenchments, load machine-gun belts, refuel (by hand) a number of B-17 Flying Fortresses en route to Manila with a stopover at Wake, haul ammunition, and carry out a score of additional chores.

All this was done without the aid of proper mechanical equipment, although bulldozers, pile drivers, and road scrapers were used extensively by the contractor's men. Civilian chief engineer Teters, a six-footer who had been a football star at the University of Washington and a combat infantry sergeant in World War I, had wanted to help the Marines. His bulldozers and digging machinery could have saved many man-hours of backbreaking work.

Devereux had asked permission to employ the civilians from Admiral Claude C. Bloch, the Fourteenth Naval District Commandant, at Pearl Harbor. The admiral radioed "negative" to the request.

"Civilians are not to do any work on defensive installations," he ordered. "This is purely a Navy task and only Navy personnel may handle ordnance. Civilians are on Wake to put up buildings, dredge the lagoon, complete the airfield and make roads."

The authorities at Pearl Harbor clung to peacetime regulations rather than accept emergency measures. As a result, instead of drilling and perfecting their skill with the guns, Wake's defenders were relegated the work of stevedores and laborers.

Luckily, the 1st Marine Defense Battalion had been given rigid training in Hawaii, and though many Marines were fresh-faced recruits, there were a number of old-timers among them, including World War I veterans and experienced campaigners who had seen action in Nicaragua, Haiti, and elsewhere.

"Not even the slaves who built the pyramids worked harder than we did on Wake. Fifteen to twenty hours a day was standard for us," a Marine private recalled. "We had neither rest, recreation nor respite for weeks at a stretch."

Devereux's men were housed in the rugged civilian quarters at Camp No. 1. There, they struggled against rats, leaky roofs (Wake had a spell of unusually wet weather with one rain squall following another, almost daily), miserable food, and uncomfortable lodgings. In sharp contrast, the civilian workers lived well. Camp No. 2 was stocked with such luxuries as cold beer, steak, ice cream, hot showers, soft mattresses, radios, recreation rooms, and movies every night. Supply ships, which the Marines unloaded, brought the latest Hollywood films for the construction workers.

"I began to hate the sight of civilians. You can get plenty jealous of a man with a fat pay check who has all the comforts of home while you're being paid only twenty-one bucks a month and getting pushed around in the bargain," a young Marine griped.

After about a month of unrelenting toil, the Marines had all their guns emplaced. The .50-caliber AA machine guns were positioned to protect the 5-inch and 3-inch batteries, and .30-caliber machine guns commanded the beach approaches. The searchlight units at Toki Point on Peale Island and Kuku Point on Wilkes Island could sweep out to sea, throwing their powerful beams for miles.

The defensive perimeter was deployed as follows:

PEACOCK POINT—(Wake Island):
Battery A: Two 5-inch guns, commanded by 1st Lt. Clarence A. Barninger. *Battery E:* Four 3-inch AA guns (only three were effective; one gun lacked a range finder),

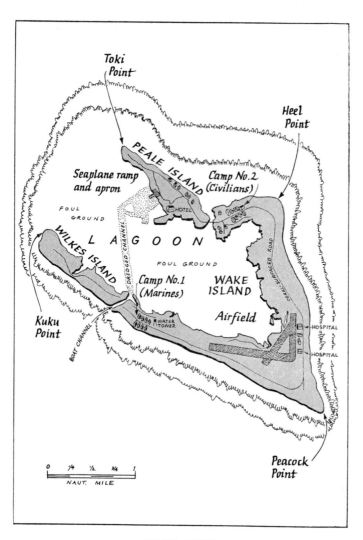

WAKE ATOLL

commanded by 1st Lt. Wallace W. Lewis.

TOKI POINT—(Peale Island):
Battery B: Two 5-inch guns, under 1st Lt. Woodrow Kessler. *Battery D:* Four 3-inch AA guns (only three guns could be manned due to lack of personnel), under Captain Bryghte D. Godbold, who also commanded Peale Island.

KUKU POINT—(Wilkes Island):
Battery L: Two 5-inch guns, under 2nd Lt. J. A. McAlister. *Battery F:* Four 3-inch AA guns (there was no personnel for this battery).

AIRFIELD—(Wake Island):
.50-caliber AA machine guns and .30-caliber machine guns served by nineteen Marines under 2nd Lt. R. M. Hanna.

HEEL POINT—(Wake Island):
Nine Marines with rifles and two .30-caliber machine guns.

In addition, there were four .50's on Wilkes Island; four on Wake at Peacock Point; four, plus a number of .30-caliber machine guns, on Peale.

The Wake defenses were completed December 3, 1941, when twelve Wildcat (F4F-3) fighter planes from Marine Fighter Squadron VMF-211, landed on Wake after taking off from the aircraft carrier *Enterprise,* which had steamed to within 100 miles of the atoll. Squadron 211 was led by Major Paul Putnam.

The Wildcats, an obsolete type, were without armor, leakproof gasoline tanks, or radio homing equipment. Putnam's fliers were green. Except for the CO and one or two others, not a single pilot of Squadron 211 had had any experience with the F4F's. Not a man had ever dropped a bomb from one or fired its machine guns. When talking about his unskilled fledglings, Putnam growled, "They'll have to learn the hard way, which is the only way for a Marine to learn anything."

A few days before the Wildcats flew in, Commander Winfield Scott Cunningham came with a small party of sailors and a few petty officers to take over the projected Naval Air Station (NAS) from which Catalina (PBY) patrol bombers were to fly, although no PBY's were available for at least several months.

Cunningham, who outranked Major Devereux, took over as atoll Commander. On December 4 (because Wake lay west of 180° longitude, beyond the International Date Line, it was a day later there than in the United States or Hawaii) Cunningham and Devereux spent many hours inspecting the defensive positions. They visited all the batteries and machine-gun posts. Both noted unhappily that the airfield had no underground gasoline installations, no tool sheds and work shops, no revetments or dispersal areas for the twelve Wildcats lined up at intervals on the airstrip. It was an inviting target for enemy planes.

Since Wake had no radar to warn of an approaching enemy, a constant watch was kept from atop a 50-foot water tower. Sirens for air-raid warnings had not yet reached the atoll. In the interim, three rapid shots in the air fired by a sentry was the signal that hostile planes had been sighted.

During the fatal first week of December, 1941, there were on Wake 449 Leathernecks, broken down to 27 Marine officers and 422 men; 10 naval officers, 58 seamen (counting hospital corpsmen); an Army communications team (1 officer and 4 enlisted men); about 70 Pan American employees; and 1,146 civilian workmen. Neither the civilians nor the Army and Navy detachments were armed.

Devereux and Cunningham were worried about their ability to hold Wake in the face of a determined attack. Both were aware of a recently arrived dispatch from Pearl Harbor which had warned that the international situation was deteriorating rapidly and that war with Japan appeared imminent.

After a long silence, Devereux said, "Well, I guess we're as ready as we'll ever be."

Cunningham nodded in glum agreement.

And over on Peale Island, a Marine in Battery D re-

read a dog-eared letter from his girl friend. He had been carrying it around since the day he left Pearl Harbor in October. The letter read in part:

". . . and darling, as long as you have to be away, I'm so happy you're in the Pacific, where you won't be in any danger if war comes. . . ."

The Leatherneck sighed and stared out at the restless sea. He listened to the resounding surf. Somewhere beyond the horizon, perhaps at this very moment, the Japanese were getting ready to strike. He crumpled the letter into a ball and tossed it away. Civilians didn't know the score; they just didn't know . . .

3. *"This is no drill"*

On Sunday, December 7, 1941, Wake time (which was Saturday, December 6, in Hawaii), Major Devereux made an announcement to his men after the morning flag-raising ceremony. They were to have the whole day off. The only work details were sentry duty on the water tower to look out for aircraft, and sufficient men to serve one gun in every battery.

The Leathernecks cheered their CO. Soon, men were swimming, playing ball, lolling on the sand, writing letters, reading, or sleeping. Some went out fishing in the launch used to cross the 50-yard-wide channel between Wake and Wilkes. One group drove in jeeps over the coral road linking Wake to Peale and snared birds there.

However, not everybody took the day off. The pilots of Squadron 211 were busy with their Wildcats, learning all about the aircraft. As if it were not enough that his pilots were new at the game, Major Putnam found that he had inherited another irksome problem. Someone at Pearl Harbor had "goofed" when ordering 100-pound aerial bombs for Wake Island. Ordnance sent bombs that did not fit the racks of Squadron 211's obsolete F4F's.

A Wildcat was designed to carry two 100-pounders, but without proper fittings on the planes, the bombs stored in magazines near the Wake Island airfield were useless. First Lieutenant John F. Kinney, aided by Sergeant-Pilot Bill Hamilton, improvised bomb racks out of scrap metal for the Wildcats.

Before sunset, Kinney and Hamilton had rigged a workable device to each of the dozen Wildcats. Onlookers praised them lavishly.

"Necessity is the mother of invention," Kinney said modestly and was promptly dubbed "Mother Necessity."

At dusk, a westbound Pan American plane, the Philippine Clipper, en route to Guam and Manila, piloted by Captain John H. Hamilton and carrying twenty passengers, put down in the lagoon off Flipper Point on Peale Island for refueling and an overnight stop at the hotel.

No one on the atoll then realized that this was to be

the last day of peace in the Pacific. Far out at sea, a powerful Japanese fleet, which included two big battleships and six aircraft carriers, escorted by destroyers and cruisers, was approaching Pearl Harbor.

Aboard the carriers, pilots had assembled for last-minute instructions and Vice Admiral Nagumo from his flagship *Akagi* signaled by blinker light: "The Emperor is watching. . . . May you succeed in your heroic efforts. . . . The cream of our Navy has been gathered for this assault. . . . We must not fail! Heaven will bear witness to the righteousness of our struggle! *Banzai!*"

And that Sunday evening, December 7 (Saturday, December 6, in Pearl Harbor), Admiral Inouye, at Truk, received a message from Admiral Yamamoto: "The Divine Wind blows tomorrow."

This meant that X-Day was to be Monday, December 8 (Sunday, December 7, Pearl Harbor time). The glorious hour had come. Inouye assembled his staff and gave them the news for which they had been waiting. Messages flashed to airfields on Roi and Namur islands of Kwajalein Atoll alerting the Twenty-fourth Air Flotilla for preinvasion strikes against Wake. Orders went to naval units to attack Guam, which was lightly defended by only a few U. S. Marines and a poorly armed island constabulary.

The unsuspecting men on Wake reluctantly watched the sun go down. They had enjoyed fine weather—not

a single rain squall had marred their pleasure. "We sure hated to see that Sunday end. We'd be right back at work in the morning," a Marine mechanic said.

At 0650 (6:50 A.M.), Monday, December 8 (then 0920—9:20 A.M.—Sunday, December 7, at Pearl Harbor), sleepy Marines were streaming into their ramshackle mess hall for an unappetizing breakfast of powdered eggs and creamed chipped beef on toast, which they called S.O.S.—"Slop on a Shingle." Major Devereux was shaving in his quarters. The Philippine Clipper had roared off for Guam at daybreak with its passengers. Civilian workmen had started their day's labor. Pile drivers *thunked;* bulldozers growled; road scrapers clanged and clattered; and dredging machines huffed in the lagoon.

A panting runner dashed into Devereux's room. He saluted and handed the major a dispatch. "Radio says it's urgent, sir," the runner said.

Major Devereux read the message at a glance. It was from Pearl Harbor: HICKHAM FIELD HAS BEEN ATTACKED BY JAP DIVE BOMBERS. THIS IS THE REAL THING.

Devereux wiped the lather from his face with a towel. "You're damn right it's urgent," he told the gawking runner. "We're at war!"

The Marine CO ran to his CP, where First Sergeant Paul Agar was on duty. Devereux shouted, "It's started! The Japs've hit Pearl! Get Field Music here on the double." (In the Marines, a bugler was called Field Music.)

Agar muttered a curse. "I always hated Mondays," he said, and reached for the telephone.

A few moments later, Field Music Alvin Waronka reported to Devereux. "Sound 'Call to Arms,' " Devereux snapped.

"Another drill, Major?" the bugler asked.

"This is no drill, son! It's war!" Devereux said. "Now, sound 'Call to Arms'!"

"Yes, sir!" The bugler gulped and dashed outside.

Waronka blew "Call to Arms" and the urgent notes shrilled over the encampment. Marines dropped mess kits, grabbed rifles, and dashed for their positions. Trucks raced away with ammunition for the 5-inch and 3-inch guns. Telephones jangled in battery CP's and the word spread across the atoll.

Some civilian workmen, gripped by panic, bolted into the brush and started digging foxholes. They abandoned bulldozers and road scrapers, flung aside tools, and fled blindly. Foreman Teters tried to halt the stampede. He kicked, punched, and cursed the men. A few emerged, shame-faced, from hiding places, but most remained cowering in the foliage.

Not every civilian behaved in such a disgraceful fashion. One burly carpenter rushed up to Major Devereux and saluted smartly. "I'm Tom Adams, former

Seaman United States Navy, sir! Can you use me?" he said.

Other workers with military experience reported to the CP and volunteered to fight. Devereux assigned Sergeant W. A. Bousher, and three civilians who had been Navy gunners, to serve the unmanned 3-inch AA gun of Battery D on Toki Point. Rifles, pistols, and hand grenades were broken out and distributed to those who asked for weapons.

The Army and Navy personnel were armed and deployed into the defense perimeter. At 1000 (10:00 A.M.), Wake time, the Philippine Clipper returned. After learning about Pearl Harbor by radio, Captain Hamilton had turned back instead of continuing to Guam, which lay 1,300 miles nearer Japan.

The Pan American pilot offered to take out his ship on a 100-mile patrol around Wake if given fighter escort. Major Putnam agreed, and the tedious task of refueling the Philippine Clipper got under way. Putnam also sent up four Wildcats to provide air cover. The remaining eight F4F's stood lined up at the airstrip, armed and ready to take off at a moment's notice.

Wake was on its toes, with nothing left to do but await the enemy.

4. *"Their wheels are dropping off!"*

EVEN AS THE Americans were bracing for the opening Japanese blows, thirty-six 2-engined Mitsubishi medium bombers ("Bettys") roared off landing strips on Roi and Namur islands, some 600 miles south of Wake. The planes, each carrying a capacity bomb load of 1,765 pounds, deployed into three neat V formations of a dozen each as ground crews waved Rising Sun flags and made themselves hoarse shouting, *Banzai!* Admiral Inouye anxiously awaited word that his "warbirds" of the Twenty-fourth Air Flotilla had started the mission. When it came, he drank a toast to their "total success" with his staff officers.

As the Bettys sped toward Wake at almost 250 mph, Japanese naval landing units, supported by destroyers, came ashore on Guam where the U. S. Marine garrison and the native police resisted gallantly for 72 hours.

And almost 3,000 miles to the east, the big ships of the U. S. Pacific Fleet, victims of the treacherous Japanese carrier plane onslaught, lay burning and twisted along Battleship Row in Pearl Harbor.

The descriptions of havoc radioed back by the attack planes indicated that the surprise raid on the American naval base had achieved results even beyond the most sanguine expectations of Premier Tojo, Admiral Yamamoto, and the *Kodo-Ha* men who had master-minded the thrust.

Perhaps, as he sat in his CP, tensely set for the enemy move against Wake, Major Devereux remembered a day in early November when the same Pan American Clipper now being prepared for flight in the lagoon had landed with the Japanese diplomat Saburo Kurusu then en route to Washington, D.C., for peace talks with the U. S. Secretary of State, Cordell Hull. At that time, before Cunningham's arrival, Devereux was still CO of the atoll and had officially welcomed Kurusu to Wake; a Marine Guard of Honor had met the Mikado's emissary at the seaplane ramp, affording him the honors customarily shown a foreign dignitary.

Kurusu, who was married to an American, graciously

acknowledged the ceremonies. He told the reception committee in a brief speech that his sole aim was "the preservation of a just peace which would cement . . . a permanent understanding between the United States and Japan."

Now, a month later, the two nations were at war. But this was not the moment to mull over the ironies of international diplomacy. Devereux had much more to occupy him than dwelling upon such matters. Grave problems confronted the Marine CO.

He fretted over the lack of manpower; wide gaps yawned in the perimeter. Instead of 900 men, he could muster only slightly more than 400, and the defense line was drawn thin. Devereux worried about ammunition shortages, the lack of radar to detect approaching planes, the dearth of medical supplies and spare parts for the planes. Wake's Leathernecks were in a tough spot; any hope of reinforcements seemed slim. Fragmentary radio reports from Pearl Harbor were all black. From what Devereux had heard, the U. S. Pacific Fleet appeared to have been practically wiped out.

But U. S. Marines had known tight places since the first Leatherneck signed the muster roll. No course remained but to face things as they came. Devereux was pleased that his men's morale was unshaken despite the mass hysteria of the civilian workers.

He remembered a squad of Leathernecks waiting to

board a truck for Toki Point watching the workers fleeing in all directions. "I never saw those guys move so
fast except to get chow or collect their pay," a Marine
laughed.

"Yeah! Look at 'em go! I'll bet they're being served
T-bone steaks smothered in mushrooms and handed a
fat Christmas bonus the way that bunch is making
tracks," another said.

A Leatherneck detail heading for a .30-caliber machine-gun position on the beach marched past the CP
as Devereux watched from the doorway. They were in
high spirits. A grinning youth called to the CO, "Hey,
Major! How does a guy get transferred from this outfit?"

"I don't belong here, Major!" a gangling Marine private snickered. "I'm allergic to bullets!"

So they went to war, these very young men—many
still in their teens. They were warriors ignorant of war.
Few had ever seen violent death. Combat, to them, was
a glittering adventure. But the tinsel would soon wear
off. Before long, each one of them would know all about
war. Some were fated to die that same day in defense
of the lonely outpost.

The morning hours passed slowly. The Marines stirred
uneasily at their guns, and the waiting became unbearable. Sentries atop the water towers scanned the empty
sky and muttered, "Why don't they come?"

At about 1100 (11:00 A.M.) heavy, black rain clouds

closed in. Thunder growled fretfully and lightning flickered. The clouds blotted out the sun and a strong wind came up, driving the surf against the coral reef with a roar. The noise of the waves was so loud that it became necessary to shout in order to be heard. As wind and waves reached their crescendo, a tropical rainstorm broke on Wake.

The downpour blinded the plane spotters; it was impossible to see more than a few yards through that driving curtain. Breakers crashed furiously against the coral, hurling frothy spume high into the air. The sudden squall ended at 1150 (11:50 A.M.), but the thick clouds still lingered and visibility was limited. The din of the waves never abated, and nobody detected the approaching drone of the thirty-six Japanese aircraft, concealed from view in the billowing clouds.

By 1158 (11:58 A.M.) the Bettys were over Wake. They dived down out of the overcast and leveled off at 2,000 feet. Only then were they spotted by a Marine sentry on one of the water towers. He responded at once by firing the three signal shots, but it was too late for defensive action.

The Japanese bombers headed straight for the airfield and the eight parked Wildcats. Within seconds, four of the grounded planes had vanished in smoke and flames. Three others caught fire, and the surviving F4F was holed by bomb fragments. As the Japanese swung away toward Peale Island, twenty-three Marine officers and enlisted men were left dead or dying; eleven others received wounds.

The Bettys swept down on the Pan American station where the Clipper passengers were lunching at the hotel. One civilian who saw the planes coming cried, "Something's wrong! Their wheels are dropping off!"

A few seconds later, he realized that bombs and not wheels were falling from the aircraft. The Bettys demolished the hotel, wrecked the Pan American radio transmitter, and destroyed almost all the facilities at the air station. The Philippine Clipper was riddled by machine-gun bullets but not seriously damaged. Ten civilians were killed in that swift raid.

By 1210 (12:10 P.M.) the initial attack on Wake was over. A spatter of AA fire did no harm to the Japanese, and the Bettys flew off, the pilots grinning, waggling their wings triumphantly as they looked back at the smoke rolling up from shattered Wake . . .

5. "I'm an American, isn't that enough?"

EMERGENCY MAKESHIFT FIREFIGHTING crews went into action on Wake Island to extinguish the flames consuming the Wildcats; over on Peale, prodigious efforts were made to put out the conflagration there. The wounded were gathered in the unfinished naval hospital, where Lieutenant (jg) Gustav Kahn, a Navy doctor, and the contractors' physician, Dr. L. S. Shank, assisted by Navy corpsmen, attended to the injured.

Major Devereux and Commander Cunningham made a quick survey of the damage that had been sustained. The most serious loss had been suffered by Squadron 211. But Lieutenant Kinney and Sergeant Hamilton went to work salvaging the wrecked planes. According to Major Putnam, ". . . they traded parts and assemblies . . . until not one aircraft could be identified. . . . They swapped engines, stripped and rebuilt them."

By nightfall of December 8, Kinney and Hamilton had made one of the damaged ships flyable. Added to the four Wildcats that had been on patrol, the Wake air force now numbered five out of the original dozen. The same cloud cover that had enabled the Japanese to sneak in unnoticed had also served to conceal them from the Wildcats.

"Luck was riding with the Nips," declared one of the patrol pilots. "If we'd spotted the raiders, we'd have jumped 'em and tumbled a few. At least the Nips wouldn't have gotten away without a scratch."

There was intensive activity all over the atoll during the hours after the attack and throughout the night of December 8–9 (Wake time). The Leathernecks and a few dozen civilian volunteers repaired bomb damage, built revetments, and filled sandbags for gun emplacements. Dynamite charges were laid along the airstrip runway and made ready for instant detonation should the enemy attempt an airborne landing.

Big Nate Teters rounded up some stray bulldozer drivers who had recovered from their initial panic. The civilians pushed dirt into the bomb holes that rutted the airfield. The bombing, and news that both Guam and Pearl Harbor had been attacked, brought a number of construction workers out of the brush. Many were Chamorros from Guam, raised to a fighting pitch by the assault on their homeland. Others, both Hawaiians and native Americans, also drifted in from hiding. Some climbed aboard abandoned bulldozers and road scrapers. Many took up picks and shovels and went to work.

A few reported to Devereux for combat assignments. The Marine CO eyed a husky New Yorker who asked for a rifle.

"Why are you doing this?" the major queried. "You're a civilian. You don't have to fight."

"I'm an American, isn't that enough?" the worker said.

Devereux nodded. "Give him a weapon," he ordered First Sergeant Agar.

But of the more than 1,000 civilians on Wake, only about 100 actually volunteered their services. During the afternoon, the Philippine Clipper, loaded beyond capacity with Pan American personnel, lumbered out of the lagoon and limped away from Wake. Those left on the atoll watched the giant aircraft until it disappeared. Several wept as the last connection with home vanished.

One civilian, a gray-haired plumber from Ohio named Orrin Fritz, stammered, "W-we're s-sure l-left up t-the c-creek w-without a p-paddle."

A teen-aged Marine standing near him sneered, "What's the matter, Pop? You aren't scared are you?"

Fritz glowered at him. "N-no, I'm n-not s-scared, s-sonny. I-I've s-stuttered all my-my life!"

During the aerial bombardment, the American flag over Camp No. 1 had been torn from its staff by a bomb splinter. Devereux ordered it raised again late that afternoon. Marines snapped to attention as Field Music Waronka sounded "To the Colors" and the flag rose slowly to the top of the pole.

When the bugler's last haunting notes had faded away, Devereux said, "That flag's going to fly night and day. The only time it'll come down is when we can't fight any more."

After the ceremony the Marines trudged back to their posts. A sergeant turned for another look at the Stars and Stripes flapping in the breeze.

"I wonder if people back in the States give a damn about what's happening out here," he said bitterly.

"They'd better, pal. Maybe no one there realizes it yet, but we're all in the same boat. If our flag's lowered, it won't be too long before the Nip flag'll be waving over the Capitol in Washington unless everybody rolls up his sleeves and starts swinging," a companion remarked.

As darkness came, the embattled Wake garrison stood to its guns. Only a few hours earlier, they had been carefree boys in uniform; then, war, death, and combat were merely words. Now they had seen, tasted, and felt war. The dead were silent under tarpaulin sheets. The wounded moaned in agony. The world had been turned upside down. These youths were about to endure the ordeal that fighting men have faced since time immemorial.

6. *"I'll tell you when I'm hurt!"*

THE THIRTY-SIX BETTYS that had raided Wake returned to their bases on Roi and Namur without a single mishap; only three or four of the two-engined medium bombers had suffered even minor damage. The jubilant pilots boasted that they had "erased the Yankees on Wake."

"A squad of overage Tokyo policemen can capture Wake after the pummeling we handed the Americans," a Betty crewman noted in his diary.

The reports that came into Admiral Inouye at Truk were highly optimistic. The admiral was well pleased with what obviously had been a successful mission; but

as an old Navy man, Inouye did not quite trust the brash
fliers of the Imperial Air Force. The aviators were a
cocky breed, too full of swagger and braggadocio.

According to the dispatches from Twenty-fourth Air
Flotilla Intelligence officers, every major installation on
Wake Atoll had been reduced. Fuel dumps, planes, ammunition piles, buildings, barracks—everything had
been hit and the path opened for a landing. However,
Inouye was a conservative officer who did not like to
take unnecessary chances. Although he knew it would
not please the fliers, Inouye ordered a second attack on
Wake for December 9.

"We did not agree with the need of another raid," a
Betty pilot said, "but since the Admiral wanted it, we
raised no objections. . . . Besides, we felt the bombing
practice would do us good."

A flight of twenty-seven Bettys was made ready for
the attack, which was scheduled at 1145 (11:45 A.M.),
December 9 (Wake time). At the same time that he
alerted the Twenty-fourth Air Flotilla, Inouye flashed
an order to Rear Admiral Samakoshi Kajioka, who commanded the Wake Invasion Force.

Kajioka was instructed to haul anchor and sail from
Roi on Tuesday, December 9; the invasion force was
to be off Wake at 0300 (3:00 A.M.) Thursday, December
11 (Wake time), when a naval bombardment would
cover the landing force.

The units mobilized for the invasion of Wake were neither large nor powerful. The make-up of the force reflected the contemptuous attitude toward Americans then prevalent in the Imperial War Council. Admiral Kajioka had been given only 450 men to capture the atoll.

His fleet consisted of the old cruiser *Yubari* (his flagship); two obsolescent light cruisers, the *Tatsuta* and the *Tenryu;* six destroyers, *Mutsuki, Kisaragi, Mochizuki, Yayoi, Oite,* and *Hayate.* In addition, the transports *Kongo Maru* and *Konryu Maru* plus two creaky patrol boats carried the 450 shock troops of the Special Naval Landing Force. These men were armed with the usual infantry weapons such as rifles, knee mortars, light machine guns, and small cannon. Two submarines on the lookout for U. S. surface units ranged far ahead of the main group.

Admiral Kajioka raised the signal "All Ships Sortie!" from the halyard of the *Yubari* at daybreak, December 9. The convoy set a course for Wake amid prolonged *banzais* from ships and shore. A band played out Kajioka's vessels and the admiral acknowledged this salute from the bridge by personally leading his staff officers in a series of *banzais.*

The Wake Invasion Force was soon in open waters that sparkled with sunshine. The troops were serenely confident. ". . . everyone behaved as though on a cruise

. . . relaxed, contented and cheerful . . .," a *Yubari* crew man remembered.

As his ships plowed through the placid ocean, Kajioka reviewed the plan of battle. Following a brisk cannonading of the shore, the troops were to make landings: ". . . 150 men on Wilkes Island . . . the remaining 300 on the south side of Wake Island to capture the airfield." In the unlikely event that the Yankees stalled the attackers or even drove them back, the destroyer crews would reinforce the assault troops.

Admiral Kajioka was ready; in slightly more than 48 hours, he would be known as the "Conqueror of Wake." The admiral was so certain of swift victory that he had already chosen a name for the atoll after its surrender: *Otori Shima*—"Bird Island."

It was an appropriate name. On the morning of December 9, as Kajioka's ships were steaming ahead and the Imperial Navy submarines poked off Wake's shores, the myriad birds rose wheeling and screeching in mass terror at 1145 (11:45 A.M.) when Marine sentries spotted twenty-seven Bettys from afar and every AA gun that could be brought to bear on the planes went into action.

So many birds were in the air that "they blotted out the sun . . . like feathery clouds," according to one Marine. Hundreds of them were killed by AA shrapnel and machine-gun bullets during the furious barrage that the

Marine 3-inchers and .50-caliber AA machine guns poured up at the Japanese aircraft.

The Betty pilots, who had anticipated a "milk run," were taken aback by this savage AA fire. Their dismay grew when a 3-inch shell scored a hit that knocked a Betty into the sea. Then two Wildcats (piloted by Second Lieutenant David D. Kliewer and Sergeant Bill Hamilton) suddenly closed in on a second bomber and set it ablaze with bursts of .50-caliber bullets.

Despite the shock of realizing that the Yankees were far from "annihilated" and still could fight, the Japanese pilots pressed home their attack. The Marines lacked sufficient AA firepower to drive them off and the few fighter planes were unable to stop the enemy.

The thin defensive cordon was breached and the bombers plastered the ground installations. The hospital at Camp No. 2 was flattened in a relentless strafing and bombing attack that killed four Marines, eleven hospital corpsmen, and about fifty civilians.

The Japanese scored a crippling blow when a Betty dropped its load squarely on the U. S. Navy radio transmitter, which had been the principal communications link with CINCPAC at Pearl Harbor. The planes made persistent passes at Battery E, the 3-inch AA guns at Peacock Point, commanded by Lieutenant Wally Lewis.

The enemy failed to hit the gun emplacement but wounded several men, among them Sergeant Andrew

J. Paszkiewicz, a veteran of 20 years in the Corps. Paszkiewicz was operating a .50-caliber AA machine gun near Battery E. A bomb blew the sergeant out of his position and sent him flying through the air. He got up bleeding from a half-dozen shrapnel wounds and staggered back to his gun, which was undamaged, although the entire crew had been wounded.

The sergeant blazed away singlehandedly at the enemy planes. When a corpsman approached to give him first aid, Paszkiewicz roared, "I'll tell you when I'm hurt! Go take care of somebody who needs help!"

After about 15 minutes, the enemy broke off the attack and flew away. This time there was no exultant wing waggling. The Bettys had not escaped unscathed. Two of them were shot down over Wake and three others, badly damaged, reportedly never made it back to their home base.

Every pilot in the second raid now understood that the first attack had been a fortuitous surprise. Even the loudest braggarts had to admit that their earlier estimates of the defensive situation on Wake were inaccurate.

Admiral Inouye went into a rage when he heard the results of the second raid. "Those conceited aviators have endangered the whole operation! Even after two assaults the Yankee defenses are intact," he complained to a staff officer.

A third aerial foray was ordered for Wednesday, December 10 (Wake time). Inouye emphasized: ". . . the aircraft *must* pave the way for our invasion force. . . . In the Emperor's name, I charge you to press the attack until the foe is battered helpless."

The chagrined commander of the Twenty-fourth Air Flotilla radioed to Truk that he would hit Wake at noon on December 10. ". . . I vow that this time nothing above ground will be left standing," he assured Admiral Inouye.

7. "We're heading for Wake!"

No SOONER HAD the last Betty disappeared than Wake's defenders again began clearing away the wreckage. With the hospital at Camp No. 2 demolished, new medical quarters had to be improvised. It was decided to set up a hospital in two large underground concrete ammunition magazines, which had not yet been placed in use. Dr. Shank and Lieutenant Kahn supervised moving their patients into these bombproof shelters, which abutted the airfield and were also near the Marine CP.

Communications with Pearl Harbor were re-established by means of a powerful portable transmitter mounted on a truck. The first message to reach Wake over the new setup came from a CINCPAC staff officer. Marked URGENT it read: PERSONNEL WILL WEAR LEGGINS AND LONG SLEEVED SHIRTS BUTTONED AT THE CUFF FOR PROTECTION AGAINST POWDER BURNS.

Major George H. Potter, the Marines' Executive Officer, slammed his helmet on the ground in disgust. "If that's all they have to say, we'd be better off without a radio!" he exclaimed.

The second message, addressed to Commander Cunningham, asked for his regular report on progress of construction work. Cunningham, usually a mild, easygoing man, sarcastically radioed back: DUE TO CIRCUMSTANCES BEYOND CONTROL, CONSTRUCTION WORK HAS BEEN INDEFINITELY SUSPENDED.

"What's the matter with those guys at Pearl? Don't they know there's a war on?" growled the radio operator as he sent the CO's dispatch.

"It'll take a little time to sink in. You can't unravel red tape that fast," said Cunningham with a grin.

Although some staff officers were still mired in the morass of peacetime bureaucracy, most faced the war situation realistically. Admiral Kimmel, whose excellent service record had been spoiled by the Japanese sneak attack on Pearl Harbor, was determined to restore his tarnished reputation.

Even as bombs shook Wake on December 9 (December 8 at Pearl Harbor), Admiral Kimmel called a staff meeting in CINCPAC Headquarters. Columns of smoke still poured from the twisted hulks of burning battle-wagons along Battleship Row, where the Japanese had done their deadliest work.

Admiral Kimmel could see the blackened superstructure of the *Arizona* poking above water. She had been sunk at her mooring with some 1,200 officers and men trapped aboard. The *Arizona* and her sister battleships were lost; nothing could change that dismal fact, revive the dead, or ease the suffering of the wounded.

Never before had the U. S. Navy suffered such a shattering defeat. Gazing out his office window at the flag still waving from the mainmast of the sunken *Arizona,* Admiral Kimmel undoubtedly did not relish his position. As CINCPAC, he was responsible for the U. S. Pacific Fleet. Blame for the Pearl Harbor debacle was already coming at him from all sides. Rumor had it that both Kimmel and his superior, Admiral Stark (CNO), were slated to be replaced very soon.

Kimmel, an old sea dog, knew that the fortunes of war did not always smile. The only way for him to wipe clean his slate was to hit back at the foe.

Nine months earlier, he had warned of Japanese intentions against Wake—a prophecy that had come true.

Kimmel now proposed to aid Wake's garrison and enable the U. S. Pacific Fleet to "get at the Imperial Navy . . . with surface, underwater and air units." At the staff conference, Kimmel's aides were told to draw up a plan for "mounting a counterblow to relieve Wake and harass the enemy."

Still smarting under the foe's success at Pearl Harbor, Kimmel's staff worked overtime to prepare a counter-attack built around Task Force (TF) 14, which included the aircraft carrier *Saratoga (Sara)* flying the flag of Rear Admiral Aubrey W. Fitch, plus Cruiser Division (CRUDIV) 6 (*Astoria, Minneapolis,* and *San Francisco* and its destroyers, the transport *Tangier,* and the oiler *Neches*). CRUDIV 6 was commanded by Rear Admiral Frank Jack Fletcher aboard the *San Francisco.*

The plan also involved TF 11, commanded by Rear Admiral Wilson Brown (the aircraft carrier *Lexington;* the cruisers *Indianapolis, Chicago,* and *Portland;* the oiler *Neosho;* and escorting destroyers). The third element in the Wake Relief Expedition was TF 8 (the aircraft carrier *Enterprise* or *Big E,* a cruiser group, and a destroyer squadron, commanded by Rear Admiral William "Bull" Halsey).

The actual relief of Wake was to be accomplished by TF 14. The *Saratoga,* steaming at full speed from San Diego, California, had aboard Marine Fighter Squadron 221—eighteen FA2 (Buffalo) fighter planes—earmarked as reinforcements for Squadron 211.

CINCPAC's general idea was for Admiral Fitch to bring TF 14 to within striking distance of Wake, where he would fly off the Buffaloes, and then land units of the 4th Marine Defense Battalion from the *Tangier*.

At the same time, Admiral Brown's TF 11 would unleash diversionary raids against Japanese bases in the Marshall Islands to pin down the enemy's naval and aerial strength. The fighters and bombers of the flattop *Lexington* (known as the *Lady Lex*) were to "seek out and destroy Japanese surface vessels . . . bomb shore facilities . . . and engage enemy aircraft where possible."

"Bull" Halsey's TF 8 was relegated to the side lines in this operation, being assigned to patrol the Hawaiian Islands and to lend a hand only in the event of a major sea engagement.

Admiral Halsey, destined to become one of the Navy's best-known fighting men, stewed and fumed over this passive role, but prepared to implement the orders that reached him on December 9, while TF 8 was out searching for the Japanese carriers that had raided Pearl Harbor two days earlier.

Halsey promptly put *Big E* about and, followed by the rest of TF 8, made full speed toward Pearl Harbor for refueling. Simultaneously, the *Lady Lex* and TF 11, set a course toward the Japanese-held Marshall Islands with instructions to refuel at sea. However, rough weather prevented this and forced Admiral Brown back to Pearl Harbor for refueling operations.

Meanwhile, events moved rapidly at battered Pearl

Harbor. By afternoon of December 10, Marines of the 4th Defense Battalion were alerted for immediate embarkation aboard the *Tangier*. Their destination was not disclosed but quickly became an open secret.

"We're heading for Wake!" shouted Leathernecks who had not yet been in combat, and rolled full field packs in preparation for the long voyage out. They spent that day and the next loading machine-gun belts, hauling ammunition, uncrating cases of rifles, removing grease from spare parts, and trucking mountains of equipment to the dockside where everything was loaded aboard the *Tangier*.

Before long the transport's holds bulged with 9,000 rounds of 5-inch shells, 12,000 AA shells (3-inch), .50- and .30-caliber ammunition, spare parts, rations, and radar equipment of the latest design, just arrived from the States.

The Leathernecks waited on the dock for hours but received no orders to go aboard, and at night were marched back to barracks. Their embarkation was delayed by the tardiness of the *Saratoga* from San Diego. The *Sara* had been forced to take several long detours from her path due to reports of Japanese submarines.

Not until Sunday, December 14—exactly one week after the historic "Day of Infamy"—did the big flattop finally reach Pearl Harbor. Once the *Sara* slipped into her berth and began to refuel, more than 500 Leathernecks tramped up the gangplank of the *Tangier*. The next day she lifted anchor and, accompanied by fleet oiler *Neches* and four destroyers, moved out to sea for a rendezvous off Pearl Harbor with the *Saratoga*. At 1145 (11:45 A.M.) Tuesday, December 16, the *Sara*, escorted by CRUDIV 6, plus a squadron of destroyers, finally set sail. (Command of TF 11 and the relief operation devolved upon Admiral Fletcher, who was senior in grade to Admiral Fitch.)

Succor seemed at hand for the besieged men on Wake, where Devereux's Marines already had beaten off one Japanese invasion attempt and were girded for another.

8. *"Our lives belong to the Mikado!"*

WHILE ADMIRAL KIMMEL's staff was finding the means of helping Wake, Devereux and his beleaguered Leathernecks were helping themselves. After the air raid on Tuesday, December 9, Devereux was positive that enemy planes had spotted Battery E—the 3-inch AA guns at Peacock Point—and felt certain that the next attackers would try to knock out this vital position. Accordingly, he ordered the battery CO, Lieutenant Wally Lewis, to move his guns some 600 yards east and north along the beach.

This was a back-breaking job, for each 3-incher weighed about 8 tons. However, the arduous task of digging emplacements for them with pick and shovel was eased by Nate Teters, who brought in a crew with mechanical digging equipment.

"Old Nate and his boys sure made the dirt fly," a Marine observed. "I felt that I was on Easy Street not having to swing a pick."

The semimobile 3-inchers had to be hand-hauled part of the way when two trucks bogged down in the sand. Marines and civilian volunteers dragged cases of ammunition to the new position. They toiled all night long and, by daybreak, Battery E was ready. The exhausted men dropped to the sand for a few hours' sleep. Meanwhile, carpenters had hammered together decoy guns of scrap lumber which were exposed in the old Battery E emplacement. Camouflage nets concealed from aircraft the true deployment of the 3-inchers.

The Japanese bombers appeared right on schedule at about noon. Devereux's guess had been a shrewd one: The Bettys made for Battery E's former position and pulverized it with a hail of 132-pound projectiles.

"Had we left the guns where we originally had placed them, they'd have been pounded to pieces," Lieutenant Lewis wrote. "As it was, Battery E knocked down at least one Betty and damaged another."

The high point in the defense that day came when Captain Henry Elrod, known as "Hammering Hank," took up a Wildcat and "tumbled" two of the foe's aircraft. However, the Japanese penetrated the AA curtain to plaster the beach on Wilkes Island. During a strafing run, machine-gun bullets from a Betty blew up a construction storage shed housing 125 tons of dynamite.

The resultant blast set off all the ready ammunition on Batteries F and L and denuded Wilkes Island of brush and foliage. It also started a number of grass fires, destroyed a searchlight unit, ruined control equipment, wrecked the range finder of Battery L—the 5-inch guns —and damaged some valuable spare parts.

Miraculously, the casualties were minimal. One Marine was killed. Four Leathernecks and one civilian suffered wounds. Marine Corporal Bernard Richardson (Battery L) incurred an irreplaceable loss. Richardson, who had been in show business, was writing a novel about stock acting companies, tent shows, and carnivals. He had some 150,000 words of it completed. The manuscript, stowed in his musette bag, was destroyed by the big explosion.

"From now on," the corporal vowed ruefully, "I'll stick to writing short stories."

Another Battery L Marine, Private First Class Verne Wallace of Philadelphia, had managed a movie theater in his home town. Back in 1940, a group of friends had dared him to join the Marine Corps. After the Bettys flew off, he stood muttering aloud, "What am I doing here? I should be in Philly where I belong! God, I wish I'd kept my big mouth shut and stayed there."

Before many hours passed, everyone on Wake would long to be elsewhere. The Japanese invasion force was almost within striking distance. A strong northeasterly wind rose shortly after nightfall. Thick mists swirled about Wake, and watchful sentries stared at the shifting gray mass that limited visibility to only a few miles.

Aboard his flagship the *Yubari*, Admiral Kajioka paced the bridge and cursed at the heavy swells that made his cruiser pitch and sway. He could barely make out the signal lights of the *Tenryu* and the *Tatsuta* blinking through the milky fog to other ships in the convoy. The rough water worried Kajioka; it would be difficult to launch small assault boats. The murky haze he saw as a mixed blessing—if it cut down his own field of vision, the mist also allowed his ships to move unseen by any prowling American submarines.

After midnight, December 11, a stiffening breeze dispelled the fog and the moon came out, although the heavy seas did not abate. Kajioka summoned his staff officers to the *Yubari's* cramped chart room and went over final details. When the hour-long conference concluded, stewards moved among the assembled officers filling small silver cups with *sake,* the traditional Japanese drink.

Admiral Kajioka raised his cup high and faced the group. "Our lives belong to the Mikado!" he said and tossed off the rice wine. The others drank, then filed out of the chart room. Blinkers signaled the patrol boats (PB 32 and PB 33) carrying the storming parties.

"Alert all hands! Prepare for assault! *Banzai!*"

The wiry men of the Special Naval Landing Force went to predesignated positions. The wind moaned. Spray sloshed over the gunwales of the clumsy PB's, dousing the tense warriors who clutched their rifle barrels within sweaty palms. Surely, even these stoical Nipponese must have been gripped by the same misgivings that have tormented every warrior in the long agony of waiting before combat.

Every Japanese soldier had been taught that his life belonged to the Mikado. But he was young, and life was precious. He remembered a girl, summer sunshine, blossoming cherry trees; he remembered laughter and music, the taste of savory cooking, snow-capped mountain peaks. He wanted with all his heart to live. So the soldier hid his fears and doubts. He wore a blank mask and forced himself to believe that death in battle was his greatest glory.

He stood in the lurching boat listening to the throbbing motors, the wind, and the waves slamming against the sides of the vessels. Every second brought him closer to the unknown shore of the place now called *Otori Shima*. And he knew not if death awaited him there.

All around, in the darkness, signals winked from ship to ship across the churning waters. Gun crews stripped canvas covers from their pieces. Extra ammunition was hauled up on deck. Turret commanders plotted range and firing charts. Gunners double-checked weapons. High in crow's-nests, lookouts scanned through night glasses the adjacent waters in a constant, tense search for Yankee warships.

The time of decision was nearing . . .

9. *"Do you think this is a ball game?"*

At about 0300 (3:00 a.m.), Thursday, December 11 (Wake time), a Marine sentry walked his solitary post near Battery A at Peacock Point on Wake Island. The night was black, the silence broken only by booming waves pounding on the reef. The lone Leatherneck paused atop a sand dune and stared seaward into the darkness.

The wan moon shone through a slight overcast on the restless water; only a few stars were visible. As he surveyed the heaving ocean, the Marine saw something startling. Several miles from shore, he noticed tiny specks of light blinking and bobbing.

At first the sentry thought that they were stars; but no stars had ever hung that low in the sky. Then he decided that his eyes were playing tricks; but no matter how many times he turned away and looked back, the lights remained, dancing and weaving in the distance.

The Leatherneck called the corporal of the guard, and the noncom, scanning the sea with night glasses, agreed that lights were flashing out there. The corporal then notified the CP. Soon, Major Devereux, Major Potter, and Commander Cunningham, the atoll CO, were grouped at Peacock Point, peering through binoculars.

The lights had drawn closer by 0400 (4:00 A.M.) and were clearly discernible. A half-hour later, the watchers could make out the shadowy hulls of ships.

"It's the Japs!" Devereux said. "Alert all batteries and beach positions!"

Moments later, field telephones were jangling in battery CP's. Intercom radio loud-speakers squawked urgently. Sleepy men awakened and dashed to their posts. Commanders of 5-inch batteries at Peacock, Kuku, and Toki points took sightings and began to track targets. On the beaches, riflemen and machine gunners crouched in foxholes and squinted hard across the water.

As dawn neared, everyone saw the approaching enemy fleet. The ships, steaming in array, must have seemed overwhelmingly formidable to the Marines on shore. With the *Yubari* in the lead, battle flags flying, the cruisers, destroyers, and transports made an impressive sight. However, the laconic Leathernecks were not overawed.

"Anything that floats can be sunk," a sergeant of Battery B on Toki Point pointed out.

A gunner patted the barrel of a 5-inch cannon. "And this is the baby that'll do it," he boasted.

There was a lot of brave talk and nervous wisecracking among the Marines. The gun crews serving the two 5-inchers of Battery A on Peacock Point made bets as to which gun would sink the first enemy ship.

But the banter stopped at 0500 (5:00 A.M.) when the foe, some four miles at sea, started maneuvering for a firing run. The *Yubari* and four destroyers swung westward off the southern shore of Wake and Wilkes islands while the *Tenryu* and *Tatsuta,* with their destroyers, headed for Peale Island.

The sun had risen well above the horizon by then; the day was cloudless, but a strong northeasterly wind still caused heavy swells to thunder against the reef.

In his CP, Major Devereux was busy checking with his battery commanders. He issued a blanket order: "No one will open fire until I give the word." The slender officer also made contact with Major Putnam and found that Squadron 211 had four planes capable of flying.

"Stay down until the shore batteries start to shoot," Devereux said.

Putnam passed the word to the three pilots who would take to the air with him. He had picked only his most experienced fliers for the mission: Captain "Hammering Hank" Elrod, Captain Herbert C. Freuler, and Captain Frank Thorin. The men sat in their Wildcats, ready to go at any time.

The *Yubari* and her escorts arrogantly steamed past the tip of Peacock Point some 5,700 yards out. At 0530 (5:30 A.M.) Admiral Kajioka nodded to his staff gunnery officer, who gave the signal for the cruiser's big guns to begin the bombardment. The *Yubari's* broadside flamed and thundered; the destroyers joined the crashing chorus.

The *Yubari* cruised the length of Wake Island and Wilkes Island with guns blazing. However, neither she nor her destroyers caused any major damage. The torrent of shells ignited some oil storage tanks near Camp No. 1, but no Marine casualties resulted. At the same time, the Japanese PB's and transports deployed to lower boats for the storming parties. The heavy sea balked their efforts. Several of the launched boats, loaded with troops, capsized. Weighted down by packs and weapons, the unfortunate soldiers drowned.

As enemy shelling increased in tempo, Major Devereux was besieged by requests from his gun commanders for permission to open fire. The CO calmly told them to wait.

Puzzled by his superior's reluctance to give the necessary orders, Major Potter asked, "What's wrong, Jim? Why are you delaying?"

"I don't want the Nips to spot our guns. I'm trying to make them believe their planes knocked out our batteries. If I can bring the Japs a little closer, we'll really give them a black eye," Devereux replied.

His canny plan worked. Convinced that the Americans had nothing left with which to hit back, Kajioka indiscreetly ordered his ships to move in at shorter range. By 0610 (6:10 A.M.) the *Yubari* was again off Peacock Point making ready for a second bombardment run down the coast. As the foe swung about, Devereux telephoned Lieutenant Barninger at Battery A. "It's all yours, Barny," he said. "Lay it on the line!"

This was what Barninger wanted to hear. He made a quick check of range and elevation. When the Japanese flagship appeared in his gunsights, the lieutenant yelled, "NOW!"

The 5-inchers spoke. Two hits shook the *Yubari*, and then two more shells exploded on the enemy cruiser. Flames enveloped the stricken ship. She limped away over the horizon, behind a protective smoke screen sent up by the escort destroyers.

A little later, Battery L on Wilkes Island opened on the *Hayate*, which led two other destroyers. The guns, sighted by Battery CO McAlister, struck the *Hayate* in

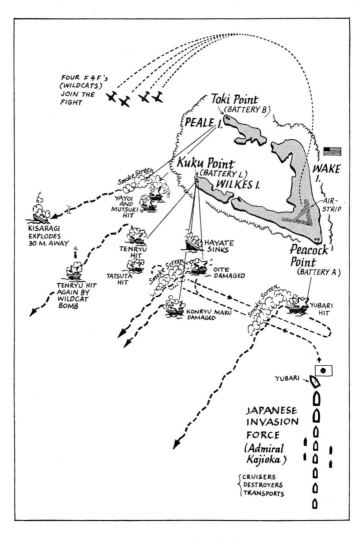

DECEMBER 11, 1941

a vital spot. She blew up, broke in two, and sank with all hands at 0652 (6:52 A.M.).

When the enemy destroyer exploded, Battery L's gunners broke off firing for a spontaneous celebration. The men cheered, laughed, whacked one another on the back, and turned handsprings. But a granite-jawed Marine veteran, Platoon Sergeant Henry Bedell, squelched their high-jinks.

"Get back to the guns, you damn fools! Do you think this is a ball game?" he bellowed.

The chastened Leathernecks scurried to work again. They mollified the bristling sergeant by immediately hitting the destroyer *Oite* and damaging the transport *Konryu Maru,* causing casualties on both ships. The cruiser *Tenryu* was the next victim; she dropped out of the fight trailing clouds of smoke. Later a Marine said, "The Japs scrammed because they were afraid Bedell would holler at them!"

Three Imperial Navy destroyers, *Yayoi, Mutsuki,* and *Kisaragi,* ventured within range of Battery B on Toki Point, where Lieutenant Woodrow Kessler commanded the 5-inchers. The *Yayoi,* which was leading, took a salvo and staggered off. The *Mutsuki* and the *Kisaragi* stood fast and raked the Peale Island bastion with a barrage. Japanese shells rained all around Battery B, damaging its control communications, but after a hot fight, those two ships also turned tail.

While all this action was going on, Putnam, Freuler, Thorin, and Elrod took off in their F4F's. The Wildcats dropped 100-pounders from the makeshift releases and swept low to strafe the harried enemy. A bomb put the torpedo battery of the *Tenryu* out of action, and another demolished the radio room of the *Tatsuta*.

"Hammering Hank" Elrod's plane was hit by flak from the crippled *Kisaragi*, yet he managed to drop a 100-pounder squarely amidships on the hapless destroyer. With his plane burning and almost out of control, Elrod crash-landed on the airstrip. The plane was completely destroyed but the pilot walked away from the wreckage.

"Honest, guys, I'm sorry as hell about the plane," Elrod said as corpsmen raced up to give him medical assistance that he did not need.

When the Wildcats completed this mission and came down to refuel and rearm, it was discovered that Captain Freuler's engine had been pierced by flak. Despite this, he tried to go up again, only to crash on the take-off. Luckily, he emerged uninjured.

With only two planes in usable condition, Putnam substituted Lieutenant Kinney and Sergeant Hamilton for Freuler and Thorin.

At 0731 (7:31 A.M.), Kinney sighted the maimed *Kisaragi* and circled for an attack. Just as he was about to release his bombs a great explosion rent the ship.

"Bits and pieces flew high in the air and a sheet of fire shot 'way up," Kinney later reported. "When I looked down, there was nothing left of the destroyer except a few pieces of wreckage floating on the surface."

The doomed ship had been carrying an extra load of depth charges on her deck. Apparently, Elrod's bomb had set off those lethal missiles. This was the last act of the first Japanese invasion effort. Only a minute before the *Kisaragi* disappeared without survivors, Devereux had ordered a cease-fire, for the foe was in full retreat.

One of Kajioka's staff officers explained the Japanese retirement: "because . . . we had already suffered losses and the defense guns were very accurate, the Admiral decided, at 0700, to retire to Kwajalein and make another attempt when conditions were more favorable."

This bland statement sought to cover up an ignominious defeat for the Imperial Navy. Admiral Kajioka's losses were large: 2 destroyers sunk, 7 ships damaged, about 500 men killed, and an unknown number wounded. The Americans came out of the engagement almost unscathed. Their casualties totaled only one Marine killed and four wounded. The defenders had lost two planes and the damage to the control communications in Battery B which hampered the operation of those guns.

The beleaguered Marines still had plenty of fight left.

At noon, eighteen Japanese bombers appeared. The remaining Wildcats shot down two Bettys, AA guns accounted for another, and four more were seen to fly away trailing smoke.

Nor was Squadron 211 finished with the enemy. Late in the afternoon, one of the Japanese submarines that had preceded the Wake Invasion Force suffered a mechanical breakdown, which forced it to come up for repairs. While the sub was surfaced, a Marine pilot, Lieutenant Kliewer, happened to be on patrol in his F4F.

A deeply religious man, Kliewer had grave doubts over the propriety of taking human life, even in wartime. According to a friend, he had joined the Marines as a flier only because he loved planes. Yet, when he saw the enemy submarine, Kliewer hesitated barely a moment before hitting it with a 100-pound bomb. The sub disintegrated into a thousand pieces.

Upon his return, Kliewer reported to Major Putnam. Squadron 211's CO comforted the troubled young pilot. "Don't feel too bad, Dave. During a war we all must do many things that go against our natures."

"I know, Major. . . . What worries me is how easily I abandoned all my principles," Kliewer replied.

December 11 came to a close. It had been a memorable day for the Marines. Never again during the fighting in the Pacific would coast defense guns succeed in stopping an amphibious landing. The Leathernecks were justifiably elated, and one of them expressed his pride to Major Devereux as the CO came by on an inspection tour.

"We had quite a day, didn't we, Major? Quite a day!" The boyish Marine grinned.

"That's right, son," Devereux agreed.

The Leatherneck sighed. "Golly, I hope I live long enough to tell my grandchildren about it."

10. *"I'm praying, you idiot!"*

THOUGH PLEASED BY their victory, the Marines had no illusions about the future. No one doubted that the enemy was coming again, the next time in greater force. Devereux eagerly read every communiqué from Pearl Harbor, hopeful for word that help would soon come.

The only indication that the U. S. Navy had not written off Wake was the presence of two Pacific Fleet submarines—the *Tambor* and the *Triton*—in the waters around the atoll. The undersea craft were supposed to "lend all possible assistance to the Wake garrison . . . by attacking enemy shipping . . . and reporting enemy movements . . ."

For one or another reason, neither the *Triton* nor the *Tambor* was of much help. The *Triton* took the only aggressive action against the Japanese. On December 10, she fired a spread of four torpedoes at an enemy cruiser (possibly one of Kajioka's ships) but her "tin fish" missed. Although both submarines were in the area, they took no part in the December 11 fighting.

A few days later, CINCPAC ordered the submarines back to Pearl Harbor. When advised by Pacific Fleet authorities that the "pig boats" had left, Commander Cunningham tartly commented, "Who could tell they were here? A case of poison ivy would have done as much for us . . ."

During the days after the Japanese invasion attempt, CINCPAC hinted that something big was in the wind. Dispatches urged Cunningham and Devereux to be "patient" and "hold on." The two men interpreted CINCPAC's intimations as veiled assurances that substantial aid could be expected.

Even the mere promise that something might be done bolstered morale on Wake. Marines and civilians regarded every favorable whisper, every optimistic bit of "scuttlebutt," as gospel. Fanciful stories, without basis or logic, sprang up. Someone had heard that the "whole" Pacific Fleet was en route to "have it out with the Nips." Another Marine swore he had seen a decoded dispatch from Pearl Harbor which listed "a dozen Army and

Marine outfits on transports coming as reinforcements for Wake." And so the gossip went and the rumors flew.

The only news from the outside came to the Marines via radio broadcasts picked up by short wave. On December 12, only 24 hours after they had repelled Admiral Kajioka, the Leathernecks heard themselves heralded by commentators as "the defenders of the second Alamo." A Marine from Texas boastfully declared, "Yes, that's right! This *is* another Alamo! By God, it takes us Texans every time!"

He proceeded to bore everyone within earshot about the legendary prowess of the Lone Star Staters, and was promptly nicknamed "Sam Houston." After listening to his bragging for a while, a youth from Michigan called a halt.

"Why don't you rest your tonsils, Sam Houston?" the Michigander asked. "And please stop comparing us with the Alamo."

"Why?" the Texan demanded.

"Don't you know what happened at the Alamo? Every last man was killed!"

"Oh!" Sam Houston said, and fell into a morose silence.

According to one imaginative broadcaster, Major Devereux, shortly after the Japanese withdrawal, had radioed Pearl Harbor the details of the victory and al-

legedly concluded his report with the improbable statement: SEND US MORE JAPS!

When Devereux heard that one, he laughed hol-
lowly. "Why the devil would I ask for more Japs? We've
got enough trouble with those we already have!"

But back in the United States, a public, confused,
shocked, angered, and humiliated by the naval disaster
at Pearl Harbor, thrilled to the defiant (if fictitious)
words, and "Send us more Japs!" was enshrined with
such historic declarations as "Don't give up the ship!" "I
have not yet begun to fight!" and "Damn the torpedoes!
Full steam ahead!"

In that hectic period of December, 1941, newspapers
exhorted their readers to "Remember Pearl Harbor!"
and "Remember Wake!" and also revived the old battle-
cry "Remember the Alamo!" Thousands upon thousands
of youths from cities, towns, and villages flocked to
recruiting stations, unwilling to wait for the draft.

The attack on Pearl Harbor and the gallant defense of
Wake stirred Americans as nothing had since the sink-
ing of the battleship *Maine* in Havana harbor—the
spark that touched off the Spanish-American War.

Americans who had remained apathetic to Hitler's
aggressions and atrocities were outraged by Japan's
sneak blow. A wave of jingoism swept the country, and
on the West Coast, all Japanese, including *nisei*
(American-born), were moved inland to special camps.

Despite their grisly experience in World War I, Americans unrealistically believed that the nation could "spring to arms" overnight and crush the foe. They had to be reminded the hard way of what war meant. They had forgotten the admonition of Civil War General William T. Sherman who said, "War is Hell!"

The men trapped on Wake already had ample proof that Sherman was right. The day after the invasion attempt (December 12), no Japanese planes attacked the atoll. The Marines gazed skyward suspiciously. Haggard men eyed each other hopefully. None voiced the flicker of optimism he felt; perhaps—oh, let it be true—perhaps the Nips had called it quits. Maybe old Tojo had been hurt bad enough to throw in the towel. No one said it aloud, but every man knew what was going through the other fellow's mind.

That thought turned out to be wishful thinking, for on December 13 the Japanese returned. They came in greater numbers than ever. Just before noon, fifty Bettys converged on Wake. The torrent of bombs that fell exceeded anything the Marines had ever been subjected to.

The AA gunners fought back tigerishly. "I never knew a three-incher could shoot so fast," said a Marine in Battery E. (The battery had changed position again after the invasion attempt and was now emplaced about 500 yards north of its former site.)

The planes came from so many directions and skimmed so low that the .50-caliber AA gunners were firing in circles. "I was getting dizzy twirling around," a former Marine recalled. "Once I swung the gun so quickly that I clobbered one of my crewmen with the muzzle. Luckily, it caught him on the helmet, but he was mad at me for days afterwards and swore I did it on purpose because he owed me five bucks."

Bombs exploded without letup. At the height of the attack, a Leatherneck rifleman in a foxhole heard his buddy mumbling. "What are you doing?" asked the first Marine. "I'm praying, you idiot!" snapped the second. "And if you had any brains, so would you."

After what seemed an eternity, the enemy departed, bombs gone and machine-gun ammunition expended. The Marines staggered out of their holes expecting to find nothing standing and torn corpses sprawled on the sand.

Incredibly, the furious bombardment caused no casualties, although one gun in Battery E had its sight smashed, and the elevating mechanism damaged. However, the weapon was still operable. Devereux ordered the 3-incher dragged down to the water's edge and mounted as an antiboat gun, since it could now fire only in a flat trajectory.

That air assault on December 13 (the 12th at Pearl Harbor) marked a change in Japanese tactics. The number of daily raids was increased; planes came at dawn, noon, and dusk. The days blurred; there was no rest for the Marines; men stumbled about like zombies, hungry, tattered, dirty, and craving sleep.

The Marines began to gripe bitterly for the first time. They despaired of relief, and cynically called themselves the "Orphans of the Pacific" who "had no momma, no poppa, no Uncle Sam." They cursed the Navy that had "forsaken" them, the government that had thrown them on that benighted place where their "bones would bleach in the sun." The catch phrase on Wake in those grueling days was, "The Navy's coming, and so's Christmas!"

But when Japanese planes roared over, the gunners pumped shells and bullets at them and Squadron 211 still sent up its "junk heaps" to fight the bombers.

Lieutenant Kinney, Sergeant Hamilton, and a volunteer helper, Machinist's Mate First Class James Hesson, U. S. Navy, with some civilians, kept patching the planes, switching parts, propellers, and motor assemblies, and actually rebuilt four planes; it was "a miracle of ingenuity," according to Major Putnam.

Because the numerous bombings made cooking impossible, the men had to subsist on C rations, which were cached at various points on the atoll and distributed to the batteries twice a day. The machine-gun position at Heel Point (Wake Island) was overlooked

and no rations came for two days. The famished ma-
chine-gun crew was desperate for food. A civilian named
"Sonny" Kaiser offered to find some for the ravenous
Leathernecks, and went off on his mercy mission.

He returned a few hours later driving a jeep laden
with cases of rations; in addition, Kaiser brought several boxes of cigars and three bottles of whisky. When
the happy Marines questioned him about the source of
his booty, Kaiser merely smiled mysteriously. "I have
my ways," he said. He held up a bottle. "Who wants a
drink?" Despite persistent questioning, Kaiser never
revealed his secret.

The days passed, the bombs fell—and the strain became unbearable. Not only the humans felt it. Thousands of birds fluttered in blind flight, flying crazily,
colliding with each other, and plummeting into the sea.
The explosions had upset their balance. Even the rats
were affected. They ran in frenzied packs, squealing
with terror during the air raids.

And the Marines stared moodily at the empty expanse
of sea, silently praying for a glimpse of friendly ships,
unaware that they were between the jaws of a cruel
pincers made in Japan. The enemy had already laid
plans for another invasion.

11. *"The Yankees are a worthy foe"*

When Admiral Kajioka's defeated invaders fled from Wake, the shaken Japanese made for Roi with all possible speed. Once the ships reached their anchorage on December 13, Kajioka radioed his chief, Admiral Inouye:

"I have disgraced the Emperor . . . and assume all responsibility for what transpired at Wake on 11 December . . . I am prepared for any punishment you deem suitable . . ."

Kajioka's staff officers feared that he would commit hara-kiri. This was a ritualistic suicide ceremony that a disgraced Japanese performed by disemboweling himself. In order to prevent the admiral's self-immolation, the officers maintained a discreet but constant guard.

However, that drastic act was made unnecessary when Inouye enabled Kajioka to regain face by giving him another chance to capture Wake.

The admiral then called a meeting aboard his damaged flagship, the *Yubari,* to consider what must be done next. The chief spokesman at the conclave was Rear Admiral Marushiye Kuninori, Operations Officer of the Fourth Fleet. He declared:

". . . the Americans were very brave . . . Their seacoast artillery marksmanship was remarkably accurate . . . We must reassess our opinions of the enemy and acknowledge that the Yankees are a worthy foe . . ."

The operations officer then reviewed the casualties suffered in the abortive attack and assured his listeners that all the damaged ships could be repaired at Roi. He outlined a plan for the second invasion attempt; it was an example of Japanese inflexibility, for Kuninori presented the precise blueprint that had failed on December 11. The only difference was that this time the invasion force would be much stronger.

The sunken destroyers *Kisaragi* and *Hayate* were replaced by their sister ships the *Asnagi* and the *Yunagi.* A powerful new destroyer, the *Oboro,* which mounted six 5-inch guns, was added to the invasion fleet.

The crack naval 2d Special Landing Force, which had captured Guam, was rushed to Roi from Saipan.

This time, Kajioka would have 2,000 men, not 450, to do the job. In addition, the Japanese High Command, now convinced that Wake was tough, sent the carriers *Soryu* and *Hiryu* each with fifty-four aircraft to bolster the expedition. Both flattops had participated in the strike at Pearl Harbor. Their pilots and planes were among the best in the Imperial Navy. The aerial striking force was commanded by Rear Admiral Hiroaki Abe.

Accompanying the carriers were the heavy cruisers *Tone* and *Chikuma* with escorting destroyers. Vice Admiral Inouye, at Truk, wanted no more fiascoes from his Fourth Fleet. He dispatched to Kajioka the entire complement of a first-rate cruiser division: the *Aoba*, the *Furutaka*, the *Kinugasa*, and the *Kako* with their destroyers and auxiliary vessels. This impressive squadron flew the burgee of Rear Admiral A. Goto, who had supported the invasion and conquest of Guam.

On December 20, backed by this powerful armada, Rear Admiral Kajioka left Roi for Wake in the *Yubari*. Steaming behind his flagship came the old cruisers *Tenryu* and *Tatsuta*, fresh paint drying on the hastily repaired damage. A covey of destroyers guarded the troop-laden transports that followed the cruisers. Three submarines, *R-60*, *R-61*, and *R-62*, had been ordered to go on ahead of the main force for the purpose of scouting out any United States surface units.

Alone in his quarters, Kajioka pored over the new

invasion plan. According to the schedule, the landings were to take place about 0300 (3:00 A.M.) on December 23. Intensified bombings, led by carrier planes from the *Soryu* and the *Hiryu,* plus land-based bombers and big four-engined Kawanishi flying boats ("Emilys") from Kwajalein, would begin on December 21 to soften up Wake and eliminate its defenses.

The landings were to be made by PB's 32 and 33. They would run aground on the south shore of Wake Island near the airstrip. Then, six barges, each carrying fifty men, would come in, all along the south shore of the atoll: two barges on Wilkes Island; two between the end of the airstrip and Camp No. 1 and the last two near Peacock Point.

Counting the men on the PB's and the barges, almost 1,000 troops would be sent ashore. If they could not force a decision, another 500 men from the ships' landing parties would be committed.

Should these still not be enough, Kajioka had orders to beach the destroyers and throw their crews against the Americans. "You are to capture Wake at all costs. This is a fight to the finish!" Admiral Inouye had radioed Kajioka just before the invasion force sailed.

Kajioka well understood what that meant. He had a second chance to redeem himself. There would be no third opportunity for him.

He vowed not to fail.

12. *"All that can be done is being done!"*

ON DECEMBER 20, the same day Kajioka's fleet left Roi, a driving rainstorm kept the Japanese away from Wake and gave the Marines a brief respite. They needed even these few hours of rest. Enemy aircraft had been bombing them three times a day since December 13. Almost every installation above ground had been hit. The defenders were worn out, yet they still were not whipped.

Squadron 211 had only two planes left; somehow, unbelievably, these indestructible Wildcats continued to fly. Their fuselages were so riddled with bullets that "they looked like Swiss cheese," according to one Marine.

But the pilots were undaunted and unhesitatingly went aloft to battle the bombers. Putnam's men took turns taking up the ramshackle Wildcats; the squadron had suffered heavy casualties on the ground in the bombing raids. Of the original twenty-six pilots, only twelve remained.

Conditions on Wake were bad that Saturday, December 20. Battery commanders reported alarming shortages of 3-inch and 5-inch ammunition. Cartridges for the .50-caliber AA guns were running low. Food stocks began to give out and Lieutenant (jg) Kahn reported from the hospital that his medical supplies needed replenishment.

To make matters even grimmer, the civilians who had been living in the bush for nearly 2 weeks were starting to get out of hand. They raided the food caches, brawled with Marines, and fought among themselves. These desperate, frightened men formed into marauding "outlaw" bands that grew more troublesome every day. Both Cunningham and Devereux persistently radioed Pearl Harbor asking for the evacuation of the civilians.

"Those who have co-operated are magnificent . . . but the rest serve only to hamper the defense of this post . . . They are using up needed food and water . . . without contributing anything," Cunningham said in one dispatch to Pearl Harbor.

But no word had come about any immediate—or future—action to remove the civilians from Wake. The Marines had to deal with that unhappy situation on their own. Devereux and Cunningham were prepared to put into effect stringent rules including death by firing squad for anyone caught looting. The "outlaw" civilians were warned either to come in and help the Marines or else to stay clear.

"I've had enough of this nonsense," Devereux declared. "I intend to make an example of the next troublemaker who's caught."

His tough attitude had its effect. Almost overnight, the men in the bush began to behave better and food pilfering ended abruptly. However, the situation was deteriorating for the defenders. Every man knew that the garrison could not hold out much longer.

Then, on December 20, good news arrived in the form of a Catalina patrol bomber from Pearl Harbor, the first outside visitor to Wake since December 8, when the Pan American Clipper had flown away. The PBY arrived at 1530 (3:30 p.m.) and settled neatly in the lagoon where the Clippers used to land. Its presence evoked great excitement.

Dirt-streaked Marines with matted hair and scraggly beards crowded the bomb-wrecked seaplane ramp. They must have looked like creatures from another planet to the nattily uniformed, clean-shaven, eight-man PBY crew. A Marine watching the PBY men disembark noticed that the highest-ranking officers among them were only ensigns.

"Hey, guys!" the Leatherneck cried. "Look at that! I guess the big shots back at Pearl think Wake's too dangerous to send anything more than an ensign!"

"Now I'm really worried!" another Marine laughed.

The Catalina pilot had with him official mail and instructions for Cunningham and Devereux. He pointed to a bearded man in a crumpled uniform that bore no insignia of rank.

"You there!" the pilot said. "Where's your CO?"

"Right here," the man with the beard said. "I'm Cunningham . . ."

The flustered pilot saluted. "Sorry, sir! I didn't know —I mean you look—I didn't recognize——"

Cunningham waved his hand. "That's all right, son. I don't recognize myself. Come on along, and let's see what goodies you brought us."

As the atoll CO walked away with the pilot, one of the PBY crew looked about wide-eyed at the carnage wrought by the Japanese. "What's that?" he asked, pointing to some charred ruins.

"The world-famous Wake Island Hotel, sir," a Marine said. "Renowned for its luxurious accommodations and excellent cuisine. As you can see, sir, the establishment was only recently renovated to afford a better view of sea, sun, and surf."

"Gosh," the PBY ensign gasped. "You guys are really at war."

"No, no. We're only actors in a movie. Don't you think the sets are effective?" The Marine laughed.

At the Marine CP, the PBY pilot gave Cunningham and Devereux particulars of the relief expedition that had sailed on December 16 (Pearl Harbor time). The news cheered the harried men. Their spirits were raised even higher by a letter from CINCPAC which instructed Devereux to "prepare to receive aircraft by 23 December . . . and have all civilians ready for evacuation by 24 December . . ."

Devereux smiled as he read the dispatch, which he handed to Cunningham. The latter perused it quickly. "That's more like it," he said. "I always knew the Navy wouldn't let us down."

He would have been less cheerful had he known that the hastily mobilized Wake Relief Expedition was running into all sorts of unforeseen difficulties. On December 17 (Pearl Harbor time), the day after the *Saratoga* had sallied out of Pearl, Secretary of the Navy Frank Knox formally relieved Admiral Kimmel as CINCPAC. The man appointed to succeed Kimmel was Admiral Chester W. Nimitz, an admirable choice. However, Nimitz could not reach Pearl Harbor for several days, since he was then in Washington.

Vice Admiral William S. Pye was designated CINC-PAC until Nimitz arrived at Pearl Harbor. Pye, who had commanded the Pacific Fleet battleships, was a diligent, if unimaginative, officer. His own flagship, the *California*, had been sunk on December 7, and Pye was too painfully aware that the fleet could not afford to lose any more big ships—and especially any aircraft carriers.

As a result, he issued orders to the Wake Relief Expedition, calling for extreme caution. He was worried about the safety of the flattops *Lady Lex* and *Sara*, then proceeding into enemy waters. Pye's anxiety grew when he learned from Admiral Wilson Brown, commanding TF 11, that his cruiser group had held antiaircraft practice, only to find much of the ammunition aboard failed to function. This was indeed a grave predicament for ships expecting to meet land-based and possibly carrier-based enemy planes.

Admiral Pye was in a quandary; Intelligence reports claimed that the area into which TF 11 was sailing "had many enemy submarines . . . on patrol . . ." The anxious admiral ordered Brown to join CRUDIV 6, then slowly closing on Wake ahead of the *Saratoga*.

CRUDIV 6—*Astoria, Minneapolis,* and *San Francisco* plus destroyers—under Rear Admiral Frank Jack Fletcher, was having its own trouble. The speedy ships were forced to stay with the transport *Tangier* and the oiler *Neches,* which could make only 12 to 15 knots per hour. This delayed the Wake Relief Force and endangered every ship, including the *Saratoga.*

There was much tension aboard the *Sara.* Every hour

brought submarine alarms, reports of overwhelming Japanese naval units, scuttlebutt about "clouds of Jap planes from four carriers," and other fanciful tales. But to a man, the *Sara* crew, her officers, and fliers, were determined to push on. They meant to relieve the Wake garrison at any cost.

The pilots of Marine Fighter Squadron 221 were eager to get at the enemy. After all, it was their comrades in Squadron 211 who were bearing the brunt of the Japanese attacks. The men lined the rail and cursed the snail's pace at which the ship moved—by December 21 (Wake time) the *Sara* was still more than 600 miles from the besieged atoll, far beyond the range of her planes. The ship would have to sail another 400 miles before her aircraft were close enough to reach Wake.

On December 22, at 2000 (8:00 P.M.), Fletcher, concerned that his destroyers were running low on fuel, decided to refill them at sea from the *Neches*. The forward movement was slowed to 6 knots and the tedious refueling process started. After more than 10 hours' delay, the work was not finished, and the ships had lost a day in their journey to Wake.

Meanwhile, that American bastion felt the first onslaught of Kajioka's grand offensive. At 0650 (6:50 A.M.) the PBY flew back to Pearl Harbor. For a brief period of two hours, there was complete calm on the atoll. Some Marines grouped around a short-wave radio receiver that had picked up an English-language broadcast from Tokyo. They laughed derisively as the announcer described the surrender of Wake to the victorious and "unconquerable" Japanese.

"Man, some guys never get anything right, do they?" a Marine commented.

The lull ended at 0850 (8:50 A.M.), when planes from the Japanese carriers *Soryu* and *Hiryu* hurtled down on Wake. A wave of twenty-nine Aichi-99 dive bombers ("Vals"), escorted by eighteen Zero fighters, hit the atoll. They struck out of the overcast and took the defense by surprise. Luckily, the attack proved ineffective and caused neither casualties nor damage. Still, the presence of carrier planes was highly disturbing. Major Putnam flew off in one of the two remaining F4F's, seeking to tail the enemy back to their carrier, but did not have enough gasoline to follow them all the way.

Commander Cunningham sent an urgent call to CINCPAC, saying that carrier-borne dive bombers had struck. This was picked up by the *San Francisco,* many miles away, but Admiral Fletcher, in the midst of his refueling operation, was helpless to assist, and the *Saratoga* still cruised too far away.

Soon after the carrier planes departed, thirty-three land-based Bettys plastered Wake with disastrous effect. A stick of bombs straddled Battery D on Peale, knocking out the director unit. The defenses were crumbling under the merciless pounding. After that attack only eight of Wake's twelve 3-inch AA guns were still effective.

The enemy followed up this beating early next morning. Lieutenant Carl R. Davidson and Captain Herbert Freuler, flying the early patrol, spotted thirty-three Vals escorted by six Zero fighters. Freuler dived down on the Zeroes and within minutes shot down two of them. In that brief fray, he was wounded and his plane crippled. As Freuler turned back to Wake, he saw Davidson chasing a Val. A Zero came up behind and blasted the American; Davidson's Wildcat belched smoke and dived into the sea. Freuler brought in his disabled craft, but wrecked it in a pancake landing.

The survivors of Squadron 211 gathered around the hopelessly shattered F4F. They helped Freuler out and stood in silence for a moment.

Then Lieutenant Kinney threw up his hands. "That's it! No more planes! We're scratched!"

Major Putnam smiled ruefully. "Well, boys, our flying days are over. Let's see if Dev can use us as infantry."

The twenty-odd officers and enlisted men—all that was left of Squadron 211—marched to the Marine CP. "We're reporting for ground duty," Putnam said.

Everywhere on Wake, men made preparations for the big Japanese push. Extra ammunition was trucked to the batteries. Machine gunners piled up boxes of ammunition. Hand grenades were passed out. And the Marines waited.

Devereux flashed a message to Pearl Harbor: ENEMY ATTACK IMMINENT. ALL THAT CAN BE DONE IS BEING DONE, BUT THERE IS SO LITTLE TO DO IT WITH.

In a Peacock Point foxhole, a machine gunner turned to his crew. "If the Japs want this lousy place, it's going to cost them plenty."

"Amen, brother!" a Leatherneck grunted.

13. *"The enemy is on the island"*

VICE ADMIRAL PYE, temporarily designated as CINC-PAC, was beset by a thousand anxieties in the predawn darkness of December 22 (Pearl Harbor time). The burden of a decision that might cause the loss of American warships had fallen on him. Yet that same crucial decision could bring about a victory over the Japanese and at the same time rescue the men defending Wake.

As daylight tinted the eastern sky, the troubled admiral still paced his office, hands locked behind his back, head thrust forward, as though walking the bridge of the sunken *California*. He had been striding back and forth that way all night long. Sleep was out of the

98

question. How could one sleep when so many lives depended upon him?

Pye's instincts as a fighting sailor told him to send TF's 14 and 11 full tilt to Wake and engage the enemy in a no-quarter free-for-all. He had the ships to do just that. The *Lady Lex* and the *Sara*, with all their cruisers and destroyers, plus Halsey's *Big E* and the ships of TF 8 in reserve.

If ever the United States needed a naval victory, it was at that dark hour in her history. It was a time that called for reckless deeds and daring feats. Americans faced a bleak Christmas in 1941; the Japanese had humbled the mighty nation and shaken the confidence of its people. The silent, twisted, burned-out hulks at Pearl Harbor remained as dumb monuments of national humiliation.

This was the moment for an epic blow against the haughty enemy. Wake was the place for American vengeance. It was a moment for boldness, not timidity; audacity, not hesitation. But Admiral Pye was only a stop-gap commander. An all-out fight with the Imperial Navy would surely entail some American ship losses, and Pye was reluctant to give Admiral Nimitz, the permanent CINCPAC, a Christmas present of additional casualties.

At 0350 (3:50 A.M.), December 22 (the 23d on Wake), Pye received a brief, disturbing message from

Commander Cunningham: ENEMY APPARENTLY LANDING. About an hour later, at 0500 (5:00 A.M.), another distressing signal crackled by radio from Wake: THE ENEMY IS ON THE ISLAND. THE ISSUE IS IN DOUBT.

Irresolution gripped Admiral Pye. He knew that CRUDIV 6 was in the midst of refueling, a ticklish business under the best of conditions, and those that prevailed were far from ideal. Yet, Pye could not remain inactive; he wanted to do something for the Wake garrison, but worried about making a disastrous mistake.

At first, he decided to send the *Saratoga* to a distance of 200 miles from Wake where she could launch her planes, search out, and attack the enemy. This order he countermanded, for the *Saratoga* would then be vulnerable. A bit later, he called on Fletcher to have the *Tangier*, unescorted, make a run to Wake for the purpose of evacuating the Marines and the civilians. This, too, was countermanded.

During the day, Fleet Intelligence informed him that the latest available information placed at least two enemy carriers, two battleships, and two heavy cruisers with attendant destroyers in the vicinity of the atoll.

Concern for the safety of the *Sara* plagued him; the admiral doubted the wisdom of pitting the flattop against such a force. If she were sunk or seriously damaged, the Japanese might be encouraged to make another pass at Pearl Harbor and the Hawaiian Islands.

After a hurried meeting with his staff officers, Pye decided not to risk that eventuality and at 0911 (9:11 A.M.) ordered both TF 14 and TF 11 back to Pearl Harbor, thus sealing Wake's fate, writing off not only the outpost but also the brave men fighting there.

The order evoked a storm of protest aboard the *Saratoga*. The carrier's captain, A. H. Douglas, pleaded for a fast run-in by the flattop and all the destroyers already fueled. He proposed to attack, with his planes,

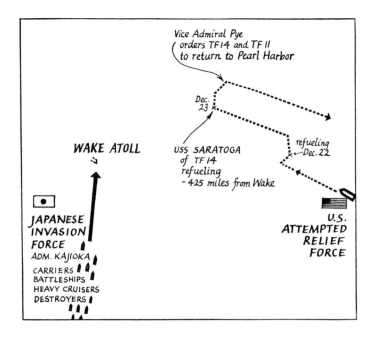

Vice Admiral Pye
orders TF14 and TF11
to return to Pearl Harbor

Dec.
23

WAKE ATOLL

USS SARATOGA
of TF14
refueling
- 425 miles from Wake

refueling
-Dec. 22

JAPANESE
INVASION
FORCE
ADM. KAJIOKA
CARRIERS
BATTLESHIPS
HEAVY CRUISERS
DESTROYERS

U.S.
ATTEMPTED
RELIEF
FORCE

every enemy ship in sight. The plan was relayed to Fletcher, who turned it down.

Marine aviators, primed to fly to rescue their comrades, cursed and even shed vexed tears. They railed and stormed, shouting their rage and frustration. The *Saratoga* rang with talk "so mutinous" that Admiral Aubrey Fitch left the bridge to "avoid hearing it," especially since "I agreed with everything that was being said," he admitted later.

But neither ranting nor wrath could change anything. The ships turned around and the task forces returned to Pearl Harbor, "licked without a fight," as an officer on the *Sara* observed.

This behind-the-scenes drama was enacted without the knowledge of the Wake garrison. For them, December 23 (the 22d in Hawaii) was slated to be merely another day of continuing ordeal and ebbing hope that rescue forces were at hand.

The day began in misty rainfall and thick clouds. The sea was turbulent and the waves boomed sonorously upon the coral reef. No one on Wake was yet aware that out in the night the ships of the powerful Japanese invasion force had been jockeying into positions for landing since 2300 (11:00 P.M.), December 22.

Admiral Kajioka's fleet had enjoyed an uneventful voyage from Roi. For the first two days (December 20–21) the weather had been idyllic: tropical sunshine and smooth water. At night, the ships sailed placidly under a benign moon and glittering stars.

"It was pleasant to sit on deck and study the heavens, picking out constellations, lulled by a gentle breeze with blue sky above and blue water below us," a Japanese soldier jotted in his journal.

The journey was without incident except for one brief, false submarine alarm; aside from that, the Japanese had not the slightest indication of any American naval units in the Central Pacific. However, the weather proved fickle and, during the afternoon of December 22, turned foul.

Suddenly, the brilliant sun was obscured by heavy clouds. "The wind rose to a furious howl . . . and screeched about the masts . . . Driving rain lashed the ships . . . From my place on the bridge of the *Yubari* I could barely see the outlines of our escort vessels . . . Huge waves washed over the prow and the cruiser was tossed about like a toy boat," one of Kajioka's staff officers noted. The storm abated somewhat by nightfall but the sea still heaved; the Imperial Navy ships maneuvered with difficulty as the admiral tried to keep them in formation.

However, while the dirty weather caused the Japanese grave difficulties, it also gave them protection from the Americans. Despite his undetected approach upon Wake, Admiral Kajioka was fearful that American submarines, surface craft, or planes would spot the ships.

Kajioka might have spared himself unnecessary anxiety. The invasion force came within 5 miles of Wake without being seen from shore. The first indication that the Marines had of its presence came at 0100 (1:00 A.M.), when sentries noticed gun flashes out to sea. The alarm was given instantly and every man alerted. The firing continued for a while and aroused much speculation about its meaning. The Americans wishfully assumed that a naval battle was going on. Perhaps the long-awaited U. S. Navy relief force had run into the Japanese and was "clobbering the Nips," in the words of an excited Leatherneck.

Nothing of the sort was taking place. An AA gunner on an enemy cruiser had mistaken some oddly shaped low-hanging clouds for American planes and started to blaze away. Once he opened fire, an epidemic of wild firing at nonexistent targets spread through the fleet. As the shooting went on, the rumor that a big sea fight was raging persisted on Wake. One overly enthusiastic radio operator even reported that he had heard a United States warship claim it had sunk a cruiser and the enemy ships were fleeing.

The rumor soon died with the gunfire. Probably every man on Wake had guessed that the alleged naval engagement was only a fantasy. At 0145 (1:45 A.M.) the hard truth was accepted by all when Lieutenant Kessler, commanding Battery B, notified the Marine CP that a lookout on Toki Point (Peale Island) had seen lights bobbing on the water. Kessler thought this indicated that small boats or landing barges were heading for shore.

This proved to be the case. At about 0130 (1:30 A.M.) the order rang out on the Japanese transports: "Land the naval landing party!" An observer aboard one of the invasion ships described what followed next:

"Without hesitation, men clambered into the storm-tossed barges . . . Officers wearing white sword sashes led the perilous descent . . . The hardships they encountered in the landing boats can barely be imagined . . . Men tumbled into the sea and were swept to their doom . . . but others took their places . . . Soon six barges each carrying fifty men . . . followed by Patrol Boats 32 and 33 with about 700 of our finest warriors made for the shore . . . the Patrol Boats scraped aground on the reef south of Camp 1 while the barges pitched towards the looming bulk of Wake Island . . . Suddenly an American searchlight stabbed the night . . . The red lines of .50 caliber tracer bullets streaked in the darkness . . . The final battle was joined . . . The death struggle had begun . . . The time was 0245 (2:45 A.M.) . . . I muttered a prayer for all the brave young men, who had so gallantly and unselfishly plunged into the ghastly hell of battle . . ."

14. *"This is as far as we go"*

THE INITIAL RESISTANCE to the Japanese landings on Wilkes Island came from Captain Wesley M. Platt and about seventy Marines at 0235 (2:35 A.M.). It was he who had illuminated the beach with a 60-inch searchlight, throwing a flood of light on the beach. Corporal Clarence McKinstry, operating a .50-caliber machine gun near the boat channel between Wilkes Island and Wake Island, immediately opened fire as the Japanese swarmed ashore, while Platt's men unloosed a torrent of rifle and .30-caliber machine-gun bullets on them.

Platt's furious barrage halted the enemy on the beach,

106

and a wild battle broke out between the outnumbered Marines and the Japanese. The fighting swirled on Wilkes Island for hours.

As this struggle was joined, hundreds of Nipponese troops began swarming off the PB's onto the south shore of Wake Island. None of the 5-inch guns could be brought to bear against these landings, and the Americans had nothing heavier than machine guns to cope with them. However, Lieutenant Robert Hanna, with a Marine corporal and three civilians, dashed down the beach and manned the 3-inch gun that had been removed from Battery E.

This weapon, emplaced between the beach and the airstrip, proved to be the main obstacle that the enemy had to overcome. Hanna and his scratch crew reached the 3-incher just as the foe's troops were climbing off the grounded PB's.

Since the cannon's sight had been damaged, Hanna laid in the piece by peering into the open breech and through the muzzle. When he had the gun lined up, Hanna commenced firing.

His first shot slammed into a PB; the improvised gun crew worked like a trained team and scored fourteen hits on the two patrol boats, which burst into flames, causing casualties among the men still aboard. The burning vessels lit up the landing areas with the brightness of day to give Marine machine gunners and riflemen a clear view of the target. A Leatherneck at Toki Point later said, "It looked like the Fourth of July."

The Japanese units that landed on Wake Island were among the best in the 2d Special Naval Landing Force —the Uchida Company and the Itaya Company (named for their commanding officers). A hundred picked men of the Takano Company had hit Wilkes Island.

The Uchidas, officers in the van, waving swords and screaming *"Banzai!"* rushed Hanna's gun. They probably would have overrun that position but for the sudden appearance of Major Putnam and the few men of Squadron 211. The fliers had been holding a defensive post near the beach, but the enemy landing swept over the small group and encircled it.

Putnam rallied his men in a charge that broke through the Japanese. During the hand-to-hand fighting that marked Squadron 211's escape, Putnam was wounded. Weak from the loss of blood, the major stayed on his feet, a pistol in each hand, shooting at the foe as his men retreated up the beach toward Hanna's gun.

Once there, Putnam shouted, "This is as far as we go!" and the fliers turned to face the onrushing Uchidas. Three or four armed civilians joined Putnam's defense line. Time after time, the airmen beat back frenzied attackers. As daybreak came, the hard-pressed Americans could see dead and dying Japanese piled up before their position. Among them were unwounded men "playing 'possum," waiting the right moment to spring up and hurl a grenade or fire a few shots at close range.

One such wily Japanese lay alongside the corpses until the Uchidas launched a *banzai* charge, personally led by Captain Uchida. As the attackers reached a screeching peak, the "dead man" jumped up and shot "Hammering Hank" Elrod in the back. Elrod's killer was riddled with bullets. At the same moment that Elrod fell, a bullet pierced Uchida's heart. The *banzai* charge stopped in its tracks and the Japanese fled.

But the pressure on the Americans was too great. The Japanese were closing in on the airfield from two sides, and Major Devereux was forced to move his CP into a half-finished bunker some two hundred yards to the north of its former position. The hospital was also evacuated and the patients carried to a partially completed building near the CP. Major George Potter, with some forty men, set up a perimeter around the hospital and the CP as a secondary defensive line.

By then, almost 1,000 Japanese were on Wake Island, opposed by fewer than 100 Marines and civilians. The bulk of the defenders were on Peale Island and the northern end of Wilkes Island. Meanwhile, small parties of Japanese in rubber boats had infiltrated across the lagoon and were moving through the thick brush. They cut communication lines between the CP and the batteries so that Devereux could not contact his isolated units and did not know the situation around the gun positions.

An effort was made to keep in touch by radio, but atmospheric conditions garbled reception and made it unintelligible. Knots of defenders fought without knowing what was happening elsewhere; some men thought that they were carrying on the battle alone.

Devereux kept informed as best he could by runners and the few places still linked to the CP by telephone. He committed his last reserves into the fighting around the airfield, sending Lieutenant Arthur Poindexter and eight enlisted men with four .30-caliber machine guns by jeep to occupy the ground between Camp No. 1 and the western end of the airstrip. His instructions to Poindexter were concise: "Hold to the last man and the last bullet."

Other Marines carried on in that tradition. Just before dawn, the Itaya Company began pressing northward up the coral road that led from Peacock Point. The only opposition in their path was six Leathernecks, a few civilians, and a .50-caliber machine gun worked by Corporal Winford J. Macanally.

These men drove the Japanese back time after time. But the enemy gradually closed in. After sunrise, one of Macanally's men excitedly called the corporal's attention to a pair of strangely clad Japanese, who were advancing at a crouch, taking cover behind some coral rocks.

"The Nips were wearing goggles and asbestos suits, with heavy gauntlets on their hands. Something that looked like fire extinguishers were strapped to their backs," the Marine recalled. "They looked like men from Mars."

Corporal Macanally swung his machine gun around and shot them. A burst struck the tank carried by one of the Japanese and it went up in flames with a violent *swoosh*.

"That was the first time any of us had ever seen a flame thrower," a Leatherneck explained.

As full daylight came, the battle-weary Marines stared, appalled: Wake Atoll was ringed by ships. The Americans saw heavy cruisers, light cruisers, and destroyers standing out to sea beyond the range of the 5-inchers. They were able to pound the atoll to pieces at will. Probably every man realized then that the battle was already lost, but this certain knowledge did not dishearten them.

The struggle raged on, although the enemy had a force ashore strong enough to overwhelm the defenders at any given point and a large reserve aboard the warships.

But the Marines entertained no thoughts of surrender. The Stars and Stripes still flew over Camp No. 1, where intrepid men had held up the enemy advance. The flagstaff had been shot in half, but a daredevil Leatherneck scaled one of the water towers and nailed the flag in place for all to see, ignoring the patter of sniper fire that slapped around him. He descended amid the applause and cheers of his comrades.

Perhaps their stubborn courage would have been dispelled had they known how dark the situation actually was. The defenders kept alive the dwindling hope that a U. S. Navy rescue force might still heave into sight over the horizon. But Commander Cunningham knew that no help could be expected. Earlier, even before daybreak, he had been informed in a CINCPAC radio message that friendly ships were not to be expected in the vicinity of Wake ". . . for at least twenty-four hours."

Cunningham did not divulge this information to anyone—not even to Major Devereux. Obviously, the dispatch meant that *no* help was ever coming. The atoll CO later explained his silence in these words: "I figured we could always surrender . . . but, as Americans, it was our duty to fight on until resistance served no further purpose . . . I did not want to prolong bloodshed, but I decided that it must never be said we on Wake had succumbed without doing our utmost . . ."

The one-sided fight raged on.

That morning, December 23, the climax of the drawn-out drama was soon to take place. Groggy from lack of sleep, the defenders blinked in the sunlight, astounded that they had somehow survived the monstrous night.

The foe was ashore in great strength, but had not yet succeeded in silencing the main centers of resistance that still held out. Savage fighting continued around Hanna's gun and at the airfield. Lieutenant Kliewer and a few enlisted men were posted there, with orders to blow up the previously mined strip if it seemed about to fall into enemy hands. Kliewer's group fought for hours. By daybreak, the lieutenant saw that he could no longer stave off the Japanese, and gave orders to detonate the charges. He then discovered that the firing mechanism was defective. While two of his men worked to fix the device, Kliewer and the others resisted the advancing enemy so effectively that the Japanese fell back.

With communications broken between the Marine CP and Wilkes Island, Major Devereux had no idea of the situation there. At dawn, the Marine CO saw Rising Sun flags fluttering across Wilkes Island and assumed this meant that American resistance had been crushed. What Devereux could not know was that Captain Platt and his Marines had the situation well in hand.

The enemy flags did not signify a Nipponese victory; they merely marked the location of Takano Company's CP. At no time did the 100 men of the Takano Company that had landed on Wilkes Island ever gain the upper hand. When the barges scraped ashore at 0300 (3:00 A.M.), bull-voiced Sergeant Henry Bedell, aided by Private First Class William Buehler, raced to the beach with a box of hand grenades. The two Marines lobbed grenades into the barges until Japanese marksmen killed Bedell and wounded Buehler.

Platt's men battled the invaders all night in a raging

"no quarter" battle. At dawn, Captain Platt skillfully led his Marines in a counterattack that wiped out the enemy. Every man in Takano Company was killed. Having eliminated the foe, Platt awaited the turn of events.

Over on Peale Island, all was quiet. A few Japanese infiltrators had come ashore, but were hunted down and killed. The biggest action there came just after dawn, when three Imperial Navy destroyers poked within range of Battery B (5-inchers) on Toki Point. Lieutenant Kessler ordered the guns to open fire, although he had only a few shells left. Hits were scored on the destroyer *Mutsuki*, which fled with the other two "tin cans." (Observers on Wilkes Island claimed to have seen the *Mutsuki* sink, but no confirmation ever was made; it must be assumed that she was merely damaged.)

Because there was no fighting on Peale and Kessler had expended all his ammunition on the *Mutsuki*, Battery B's gun crews were marched to Wake Island across the connecting coral roadway. . . .

Back in the United States, with Christmas only three days off, the usual festive spirit was dampened; a somber mood gripped the people and the preholiday shopping crowds were scant in number. Even children sensed the gloom; Christmas, 1941, was not going to be much fun for anybody.

The big stores on New York's fashionable Fifth Avenue, world renowned for their elaborate Christmas displays and spectacular lighting, remained dim and drab after dark. No bright lights transformed the city into a wondrous fairyland; wartime regulations demanded a "brown-out," which meant that electric displays were prohibited. Broadway theater signs were extinguished; the dazzling signs that had earned for Broadway the title "The Great White Way" had been turned off.

Realization that the nation was at war sank slowly into the national consciousness. No day passed without thousands of youths being called to the colors under the National Conscription Act. Drafted men streamed into hastily constructed camps, and the raucous voices of drill sergeants drowned out the Christmas carols.

Few Americans could shake off the depression that had set in on Sunday, December 7, with the raid on Pearl Harbor and daily deepened as that unhappy month dragged on.

Only the epic bravery displayed on Wake cheered the people. Every day, churches and synagogues, all houses of worship, were crowded with prayerful Americans, seeking divine aid for the men of Wake. The fate of that obscure dot of land became the prime concern of millions.

"We ask only that the courageous handful on Wake be saved from the clutches of a rapacious foe," editorialized one widely read New York tabloid.

If Pearl Harbor symbolized the country's humiliation, Wake epitomized its pride. The nation was quick to honor the Marines there. President Franklin D. Roosevelt lauded them in a coast-to-coast radio broadcast. Secretary of the Navy Frank Knox awarded a special citation to the 1st Marine Defense Battalion. The Navy Department promoted Devereux and Cunningham to lieutenant colonel and captain respectively.

But these accolades meant nothing to the men fighting on Wake. They had no time for praise; the sands were running out for them on December 23 (the 22d in the United States). Perhaps, as dawn came that Tuesday, the fifteenth day of the battle for Wake, some combat-weary Marines remembered that it was Yuletide.

Perhaps they thought of past Christmases, recalling the delight of finding electric trains under the tree or a desired bike. Many of the Marines were barely past their boyhood. Some had never spent Christmas away from home. This year there was no tree; no succulent roast turkey, ham, or roast beef; no tinsel and ribbon; no carols; no loved ones. No peace on earth and goodwill to men; only death and hardship, pain and terror.

15. *"Do you mean it, Major?"*

TUESDAY, DECEMBER 23, 1941, brought wrenching anxiety to Admiral Kajioka. He strode the bridge of the *Yubari,* pacing back and forth "like a caged wolf," according to one of his staff officers. Kajioka's temper was wolflike as well. He snarled, growled, and snapped at anyone within earshot.

The admiral's black mood was caused by reports coming in over the radio from the invasion units on Wake. Captain Uchida, he learned, was dead; Itaya company's advance up the eastern shore of Wake Island had been stopped; nothing had been heard for several hours from Wilkes Island where Captain Takano's company

117

had gone ashore. The Yankee Marines were fighting ferociously and exacting a price for every yard gained on the atoll.

Despite himself, Kajioka could not throttle a grudging admiration for the foe. How wrong the Imperial War Council had been in its estimate of Yankee fighting qualities! All those high admirals and generals must feel foolish. They had baldly stated that "Americans lacked the moral fiber and courage needed to face the descendants of samurai on the battlefield . . ." Those words must be choking them now.

Kajioka knew the difference between propaganda and truth. What his superiors told the Japanese about the Americans was propaganda; what they admitted to each other in their councils of war should have been the truth.

Unfortunately, the "brass" had actually believed their own propaganda. Instead of judging the Yankees realistically, the Japanese leaders regarded them with disdain. The triumphs at Pearl Harbor and Guam lent support to this attitude. But the "craven Yankees" were killing good Japanese soldiers on the beaches of Wilkes Island and Wake Island. The dead Uchidas, Takanos, and Itayas gave mute testimony that the Americans were not cowards but first-class fighting men.

As Invasion Force Commander, Kajioka felt responsible for his soldiers. At the very least, he owed them an honest appraisal of the U. S. Marines. They should have gone into battle fully aware that the foe was well trained, disciplined, and resolute, instead of expecting an easy victory over a demoralized enemy. They had since learned the facts . . .

Kajioka did not doubt that the Japanese would win; the odds against the Americans were overwhelming. But every hour they held out he regarded as a black mark against him. Kajioka knew Admiral Inouye was watching his every move. The Fourth Fleet CO would be more critical than usual. Inouye had given him a reprieve after the fiasco of December 11; if the seizure of Wake did not go swiftly and smoothly, Kajioka's career would end in disgrace.

The longer it took to complete the operation, the more endangered were the Imperial Navy carriers, cruisers, destroyers, and transports supporting the mission. A possibility always existed that an American submarine might sneak up on them. Kajioka shuddered over the consequences if the *Soryu* or the *Hiryu* fell victim to a Yankee torpedo.

Then, too, there was the likelihood that a U. S. Navy surface force might suddenly appear and attack the Japanese vessels around Wake. Kajioka was aware that, even after Pearl Harbor, the Pacific Fleet still had left three carriers and many heavy cruisers and destroyers.

It was logical to assume that the enemy was eager for an all-out naval engagement. Admiral Kajioka wanted no part of a sea battle. His orders had been to capture Wake, not to fight enemy ships. He had enough trouble directing the action on the atoll without having the additional worry of a surface clash.

Kajioka had hoped that once his troops had been ferried ashore they would overrun the defenses before daybreak. In anticipation of this, he had donned his dress uniform. He was an impressive figure in the starched whites, with a ceremonial sword strapped to his waist and two rows of medals clinking on his chest. How symbolic it would have been to step on Wake as the sun was rising with the Rising Sun flag fluttering over the atoll. That was a touch that would have pleased Admiral Inouye and raised Kajioka's stock with the Imperial High Command.

He had even composed a message to be radioed back to Truk: "It is my privilege and pleasure to present to the Emperor, *Otori Shima* . . ." All that remained to be added was the number of prisoners taken, the guns and equipment captured, and other details which would be included in his full report.

But by 0530 (5:30 A.M.), a half-hour after daybreak, Kajioka realized that his rosy dream of glory was not coming to pass so easily. He could have made a run in with the *Yubari* and supporting cruisers for a bombardment of Wake, but feared the 5-inch batteries. That they still carried a sting was evident—as was proved by the crippled *Mutsuki*. The Invasion Force CO did not relish placing his ships in jeopardy; the memory of December 11 was still too fresh. Of course, he could pound Wake while beyond the range of the American shore batteries, but that would impair the accuracy of his barrage.

Reluctantly, Kajioka decided to call upon the carriers *Soryu* and *Hiryu*, then maneuvering about 200 miles northwest of Wake, to launch an aerial strike with their Val bombers, escorted by Zero fighters. As did Admiral Inouye, Kajioka also disliked aviators. How Admiral Hiroaki Abe, who commanded the carrier groups, would lord it over him! How the fliers would brag that *they*, not the old-line Navy men, had humbled the Yankees.

But Kajioka had no alternative. He was forced to seek help from Abe. An Intelligence report (which proved false) reported several U. S. submarines closing on Wake. And, back home, in Japan, the Tokyo radio broadcast an announcement describing Wake's fall. The morning newspapers announced the triumph and happy Japanese were already celebrating the feat.

Admiral Abe received Kajioka's request at 0545 (5:45 A.M.); a half-hour later, both carriers launched planes. Thirty-four bombers, escorted by sixteen Zeroes—the same "Gallant Eagles of the Navy" who had blasted Pearl Harbor—zoomed through the air toward Wake, where brisk fighting still continued.

The planes arrived over the target at 0700 (7:00

A.M.). With no American aircraft to oppose them, the bombers pummeled Wake, Wilkes, and Peale islands. Almost every position was hit. Despite bombs and strafing Zeroes, Marine AA batteries fought back until, one by one, the 3-inch guns were silenced, a few by the enemy, the rest because their ammunition ran out.

Once the batteries stopped firing, the Vals raked the American lines at will. But the Gallant Eagles did not get off without losses. Riflemen whanged away at the buzzing planes and a cheer went up when a Zero crashed in a storm of ground fire.

One irate .30-caliber machine gunner, Sergeant John Cemeris, alternately aimed his weapon at three Japanese trying to sneak up on him and at a Val racing back and forth overhead.

He fired a burst at the soldiers, then at the plane. A stream of tracers killed the Val's pilot and a few seconds later the chattering machine gun riddled the three infiltrators.

Cemeris, who was a professional boxer, happened also to be a devout man, known by the nickname "Deacon," because he once had been a lay preacher.

"May God have mercy on your souls!" Cemeris cried as he turned to another target.

Everywhere on Wake, small groups of Marines and civilians resisted stubbornly. The Leathernecks at Camp No. 1 stopped a half-dozen *banzai* charges and the Stars and Stripes still flew from the water tower. But the defenders were weakening. After an epic stand, the survivors of Squadron 211 finally stopped fighting, but not until every man except one had been killed or wounded. Major Potter's scratch platoon fell back and the Japanese captured the hospital, where they bound wounded Marines with telephone wire, beat up the corpsmen, shot a civilian, destroyed all the medical supplies, and mistreated both doctors. They then pressed ahead, trying to cross the airfield. However, Potter had established an improvised line and once again he held off the enemy.

Lieutenant Kliewer, unable to put his demolition equipment into working order, retreated from the strip and managed to join Potter without losing a man. But by 0700 (7:00 A.M.) it was apparent to Major Devereux that the defenses of Wake Island were crumbling, especially after the carrier dive bombers appeared.

Devereux still had no communication with his far-flung batteries and scattered units. As far as he knew, Wilkes Island was in enemy hands, and there had been no direct word from Peale Island. The Marine CP, guarded by Potter's thin line, was coming under knee mortar fire. The last boxes of small-arms ammunition were distributed and then the supply of hand grenades ran out.

Major Devereux met with Commander Cunningham. He explained to the atoll CO that organized resistance could not be continued much longer.

"The only sensible reason for us to risk any more lives

is if there's definite assurance that we'll be getting help very soon—and I mean soon," Devereux said.

Cunningham looked uneasy. "I'm sorry, Dev. I've known for hours that we can't expect friendly ships for at least another day."

Devereux flapped his hands in resignation. "Well, that slams the lid."

Commander Cunningham nodded. "We'd better raise the white flag," he said. "There's no shame in it. We gave our best."

When Devereux returned to the CP, he told the bad news to Gunnery Sergeant John Hamos, a Marine since 1916. Hamos had fought in the Battle of Belleau Wood during World War I, seen combat in Nicaragua and Haiti, and also served in China. His reputation for toughness was legendary in the Corps. Now, this granite-hard Leatherneck had tears in his eyes.

"Do you mean it, Major?" he rasped.

"I'm afraid so, John. Pass the word to Major Potter. The string's run out," Devereux said.

Hamos wiped away his tears with grimy knuckles. "I've done everything since I joined the Corps, sir. But I never yelled 'Uncle' before. It sure goes down hard."

The burly veteran stalked out of the CP. He stood in the open for a moment, frowning at the sand. Rifles and machine guns were rattling only 100 yards away. A Japanese mortar shell exploded nearby.

The sergeant disregarded the sounds of battle. Drawing a deep breath, he strode toward the firing line and in a voice that carried above the noise bellowed, "Cease fire! Cease fire! We're surrendering! Major's orders! We're surrendering!"

16. "What's wrong with those men?"

POTTER'S MEN WERE the first to learn that the battle was lost. The word passed from one Leatherneck to the next and the firing dwindled away. But it was not in the tradition of United States Marines to surrender. Even after the order had been given, a machine gun kept hammering away at the Japanese. Potter dashed to it.

"You heard the order! Cease fire, damn it!" he roared.

"Sure, Major. I only wanted to use up this belt of ammunition. No sense letting it go to waste, is there?" the gunner asked.

The Leathernecks gave up with ill grace. Slowly, grudgingly, they drifted back to the CP and waited in glowering silence for whatever was to come. The Japanese, not yet aware of the American decision, took no advantage of the lull. Captain Itaya's company, suspicious of a trap, made no attempt to advance.

Meanwhile, Devereux spoke to all units with which he had telephonic connection. He ordered resistance to stop. Runners went out to various positions and spread the unhappy tidings. Battery D (3-inchers) at Toki Point managed to repair its phone line to the CP. Captain Godbold, the battery CO who also commanded Peale Island, asked Devereux for orders.

"Cease firing. Destroy all weapons. We're surrendering."

There was a long pause; then Godbold said deliberately, "Dev, are you all right? Is this straight?"

"You always were a hard guy to convince," Devereux replied. "It's on the level. We can't hold out any longer. Destroy the guns and come on in to the CP."

"Okay, Dev. I'd have to throw rocks at the Japs anyway—we're out of ammo," Godbold said. "I just didn't want anyone to con me into surrendering."

Captain Godbold informed Peale Island Marines. His men griped and cursed but carried out their orders. Rifle bolts were thrown into the sea and the butts smashed. They rammed hand grenades down gun muzzles. Range finders, sights, and other equipment were shattered beyond repair. One big Marine found a sledge hammer and with it smashed gun breech locks. He surveyed the damage he had wrought and grinned wryly. "I must be an anarchist at heart. I sure get a kick out of busting up government property!"

Similar actions took place in the batteries. All the 5-inchers and 3-inchers were rendered useless. Machine gunners took their weapons apart and either hurled the pieces into the sea or buried them. Then the bone-tired men plodded slowly toward the CP, drifting in by twos and threes.

However, there were riflemen and machine gunners dispersed over Wake Island whom Devereux could not reach. From time to time, shots still rang out whenever a Japanese appeared. Some last-ditch fighters heard of the capitulation but refused to give up anyway.

"The only time I'll toss in the towel is when I'm put out of action by a bullet or else ordered to surrender by Major Devereux himself," a sweat-stained officer told the CP runner who brought him the message.

Many Leathernecks expressed the same sentiment. As the runners reported back to the CP, Devereux realized that he personally had to bring an end to hostilities. He stepped out of the CP and looked about at the unhappy men grouped there.

"Don't feel bad, boys," Devereux said. "You put up a whale of a scrap."

He noticed an oldtime Marine, Sergeant Don Malleck, with whom he had served at several stations. "Don, go find a stick and tie something white to it—a towel, an undershirt, a bedsheet. We're going to visit the Nips."

"Yes, sir, Major," Malleck said. "Damn! I never thought I'd have to obey an order like this one."

A few minutes later he returned carrying a broom handle with a wrinkled bedsheet at the end. "Ready, sir," he mumbled, hanging his head.

"Come on, Don. Stand straight, man. We don't want them to think we're whipped, do we?" Devereux snapped.

The two men marched down the road toward the beach. A vagrant breeze stirred the sheet, which fluttered, for a moment, like a proud banner. They walked on past Potter's last position, littered with cartridge cases, empty canteens, a blood-stained shirt, broken rifles, discarded helmets—the debris of battle. A little further on, several dead Japanese were lying in the road.

As they neared the enemy's lines, Devereux told Malleck to keep waving the truce flag, to make certain that it would be seen. Every few steps he called out, "I'm Major James P. Devereux, commanding the United States Marines. I've come to surrender. Don't shoot!"

They saw no one, but could feel eyes watching them from the bushes. Suddenly, a Japanese lieutenant jumped out of the foliage. He brandished a long samurai sword. Behind him were a half-dozen grim soldiers with leveled rifles.

The officer shouted something in his native tongue,

motioning with the sword for Devereux and Malleck to stop.

"Do you speak English?" Devereux asked.

The officer lowered his sword. "Of course. Don't you speak Japanese? What is it you want, Major?"

"I'm here to surrender my men," Devereux said.

The officer nodded. "It's about time. I know how stubborn Americans can be. You see, I went to college in the United States, at UCLA."

The English-speaking officer sent a runner for his CO, Captain Itaya, who proved to be a roly-poly man with a benign smile and silver-rimmed eyeglasses. While the UCLA graduate acted as interpreter, Itaya explained that he would accept the surrender unconditionally. Devereux glanced at his watch. It was 0930 (9:30 A.M.).

A jeep flying a white flag bounced along the rocky road. Commander Cunningham was seated beside the driver. He had shaved and put on his best uniform.

"I didn't want to look like a tramp when I met the Japs," he recalled later.

Since he was atoll CO, Cunningham outranked Devereux and, in accordance with military custom, completed the formal surrender. Itaya's first demand was for Devereux, accompanied by the American-educated lieutenant and a platoon of soldiers, to visit every position and persuade his Marines to capitulate.

With Malleck in the van, carrying the flag of truce, the group trudged from point to point. Individual Marines obediently rose from places of concealment when Devereux called them out. At one position, Lieutenant Poindexter and his men came running with fixed bayonets, ready for a finish fight. Only a quick word from Devereux prevented a bloody clash. Poindexter, convinced that his CO was a prisoner, had intended to rescue him.

By noon, all the Marines on Wake Island had been rounded up. Japanese soldiers spread through the bush and flushed the civilians hiding there. Only Wilkes Island remained to be visited. Some sporadic firing was still coming from the Kuku Point area.

Guarded by thirty Japanese, Devereux and Malleck crossed the channel in an Imperial Navy launch. Captain Platt, the ferocious defender of Wilkes Island, spotted the boat making the passage and thought the enemy was attempting another landing.

Rallying his men, who had been busy mopping up a few infiltrators, Platt started on the double for the channel. His Leathernecks were ready to open fire on the "invaders" when Platt noticed the white flag.

He went out to meet the bearer, in the mistaken belief that the foe was surrendering to him. When he recognized Devereux, Platt cried out in dismay.

"Is it all over, Dev?" he exclaimed.

"That's right, Wes," Devereux said.

Platt signaled his men to drop their weapons. "It's only the beginning, Major," he said. "Sure, we lost this battle. But there's still a big war ahead—maybe we'll be out of it, in one of Tojo's prisoner-of-war camps, but at least we got our licks."

Later, at 1330 (1:30 P.M.), the American captives, about 400 Marine officers and enlisted men, and some 1,000 civilians, were herded to Camp No. 1 where Admiral Kajioka, resplendent in white uniform, clinking medals, and dress sword, came ashore to take possession of Wake in the Emperor's name. The American flag was ripped off the water tower and tossed contemptuously to the ground. Japan's Rising Sun was hoisted on an improvised staff amid a rousing chorus of *banzais*. Wake atoll had become *Otori Shima* and Admiral Kajioka was content.

About an hour after the flag raising, Devereux, Cunningham, and the other Marine officers were separated from their men. Admiral Kajioka ordered them served rice and *sake*. Although the American officers were hungry, they refused to accept any food until assured that their men would also be fed. Kajioka granted this request and sent his compliments to Major Devereux.

"You are a true leader . . . an officer who looks after the welfare of his soldiers . . . a foe both tenacious and noble," declared the admiral in a lengthy statement, which was read to Devereux and the officers in halting English by a member of Kajioka's staff.

The Americans shifted uncomfortably during the session. "Why doesn't he just hand out the chow instead of that junk?" Captain Platt whispered.

"They'll either starve us to death or bore us to death. And I don't know which is worse," an officer said.

But at last the reading ended. The staff officer departed after much bowing and saluting. Then orderlies came with bowls of steaming rice and bottles of *sake*. Across the camp, the enlisted Marines were lining up for rations when a group of bedraggled Leathernecks straggled in from Heel Point. Guards surrounded the famished, tired, and dirty Americans. They shuffled slowly, shoulders slumped, eyes downcast.

In the front rank was a barrel-chested, six-foot-tall Marine sergeant who sported a fiercely bristling mustache. When he saw Devereux and the officers, the sergeant turned to his fellow prisoners and cried, "Snap to it! You're U. S. Marines! Not chain-gang convicts!"

The Leathernecks came to attention and marched as though on parade, heads high, arms swinging. When they drew abreast of their officers, the sergeant roared, "Eyes right!" He saluted smartly and the detachment swung by in perfect cadence at a pace that forced the short-legged guards to trot in order to keep up with them.

An astonished Admiral Kajioka witnessed this performance. "What's wrong with those men?" he querulously asked. "They don't act like prisoners!"

Thus, with defiance still aflame, Wake's Marines went off to the oblivion of a four-year-long captivity. The civilians were taken to detention camps in China, while the Marines, officers and men, were shipped to a prisoner-of-war camp on Luzon in the Philippines. As the war progressed, they were shifted several times. At first, the enemy treated the veterans of Wake decently, but with the passing years and the ebbing of Japanese fortunes, conditions grew progressively worse, especially for the enlisted men. Some died of starvation, mistreatment, and disease, but most survived the long ordeal.

"We forced ourselves to live; we wouldn't give the Nips the satisfaction of seeing us die," said one Leatherneck survivor.

While the men who had defended Wake so bravely were languishing in captivity, the United States took up the fight for the tiny atoll. Although no attempt was made to recapture Wake, it was so heavily bombed that the enemy could make little use of the base he had so dearly bought. The war's largest raid against Wake took place on October 5–6, 1943, when planes from the biggest carrier task force organized up to that point pounded the atoll. The fast flattops *Essex, Yorktown,*

Lexington, Cowpens, Independence, and *Belleau Wood*
with escorting cruisers and destroyers hit Japanese installations on Wake. (The carriers were all newly built
ships. Two of them—the *Lexington* and the *Yorktown*
—bore the names of older vessels that had gone down
in previous battles.)

This force, under Rear Admiral Alfred E. Montgom-
ery, damaged Wake so severely that the airfield and
patrol-plane base built there by the Japanese was
immobilized for a long time. Subsequent bombings—
at least ten major raids were mounted—and shellings
by cruisers and destroyers kept Wake in a state of
shambles.

Despite all this, the Rising Sun flag flew over *Otori
Shima* from December 23, 1941, until September 7, 1945,
a few days after Japan's Premier, Hideki Tojo, had
signed an unconditional surrender aboard the USS *Mis-
souri* in Tokyo harbor.

The Americans repossessed Wake without a battle.
On September 7, 1945, a Japanese admiral gave up the
atoll to an American general. At the last moment, the
general stepped aside so that a slim, sunken-cheeked
Marine lieutenant colonel, only recently released from
a Japanese prisoner-of-war compound, could take the
admiral's sword as the symbol of the foe's defeat.

Jim Devereux had returned in triumph to Wake, acting for the men who had fought and suffered there.

The Japanese flag no longer flew from the staff at Camp No. 1. In its place fluttered the Stars and Stripes. The name *Otori Shima* was dropped; the lonely atoll again had become American soil.

Devereux noted that little had changed on Wake in his four year absence. The odd-looking rats still scurried in the brush. Clouds of birds circled, screeched, and fluttered. The surf boomed and columns of froth rose high above the lagoon. Only his Marines were gone.

Perhaps, as he gripped the surrender sword, Devereux recalled the terrible ordeal of the battle, the longer and more terrible one of the prison camps. Perhaps he thought of the bold and reckless boys who had fought so hard to hold this place of sand and coral, suffering and dying in a cause they did not fully understand, yet, somehow, realizing that theirs was the good fight.

So ended the saga of Wake.

The deeds of courage and sacrifice done there in December, 1941, were soon overshadowed by greater feats in bigger battles; the men of Wake were forgotten in the immensity of global conflict. But not even the passing years could tarnish the spirit and courage of the brave men who had rekindled American pride in a time of despair and humiliation.

BRIEF GLOSSARY OF
MILITARY ABBREVIATIONS

AA	Antiaircraft cannon
CINCPAC	Commander-in-Chief, Pacific Fleet
CNO	Chief of Naval Operations
CO	Commanding Officer
CP	Command Post
CRUDIV	Cruiser Division
NAS	Naval Air Station
PT	Motor torpedo boat
TF	Task Force
USMC	United States Marine Corps
USN	United States Navy

UNITED STATES AND JAPANESE CASUALTIES ON WAKE

United States

	Officers	Enlisted Men	
Marines			
Killed	5	42	
Wounded	6	26	
Missing	0	2	
	11	70	TOTAL: 81

	Officers	Enlisted Men	
Navy Personnel			
Killed	0	3	
Wounded	0	5	
	0	8	TOTAL: 8

Civilians

Killed	70
Wounded	12
	82

Total Killed	120
Wounded	49
Missing	2
	171 U. S. Casualties

Americans captured on Wake totaled more than 400 Marines and other military personnel, while over 1,000 civilians were also taken.
138

UNITED STATES AND JAPANESE CASUALTIES ON WAKE

*Japanese**

AIR LOSSES DECEMBER 8—23

	Killed	Wounded
4 carrier planes	4	—
1 "Emily" 4-engined bomber	6	—
16 "Betty" 2-engined bombers	80	—
21**	90***	0

LOSSES SUSTAINED DURING INVASION ATTEMPT OF DECEMBER 11

	Killed	Wounded
51 aircraft damaged by flak	13	13
2 destroyers sunk with all hands	500	—
8 ships damaged	80	160
1 submarine (unknown casualties)		
	593	173

LOSSES SUSTAINED DURING INVASION ON DECEMBER 23

	Killed	Wounded
Casualties in ground combat	125	125
Casualties aboard landing craft hit by 2nd Lt. R. M. Hanna's gun	7	25
Casualties aboard *Mutsuki*	5	10
	137	160

Total Killed   820
Wounded   333

1,153 Japanese Casualties

*   *No official Japanese records of casualties were available. All figures are conservative estimates.*

**   *This figure represents only those planes shot down over the atoll. Actual losses are unknown.*

***   *This figure includes only those bodies recovered by the Marines.*

TYPES OF AIRCRAFT USED AT WAKE

United States

B-17 (Flying Fortress)	Army, 4 engines, heavy bomber
F4F-3 (Wildcat)	Navy, 1 engine, fighter
PBY-5 (Catalina)	2 engines, patrol bomber, seaplane
F2A (Buffalo)	Navy, 1 engine, fighter

Japanese

Mitsubishi Zero 1 (Betty)	2 engines, medium bomber
Kawanishi Zero 2 (Emily)	4 engines, bomber, seaplane
Nakajima 97-2 (Kate)	1 engine, high-level bomber
Aichi 99-1 (Val)	1 engine, dive bomber
Zero-3 (Zeke)	1 engine, fighter

SUGGESTED READING

In gathering material for *Wake: The Story of a Battle,* I consulted private memoirs, ship's logs, unit journals, and other material not easily available to the general reader. However, anyone desirous of studying further about the events on Wake will profit from the following works:

Bayler, Lt. Col. Walter, and Carnes, Cecil
Last Man off Wake Island. Indianapolis and New York: The Bobbs-Merrill Co., 1943.

Devereux, Col. James P. S.
The Story of Wake Island. Philadelphia and New York: J. B. Lippincott Co., 1947.

Heinl, Lt. Col. R. D., Jr.
The Defense of Wake. Washington: Government Printing Office, 1947.

Hough, Lt. Col. Frank O.
Pearl Harbor to Guadalcanal (History of U.S. Marine Corps Operations in World War II). Washington: Government Printing Office, 1958.

Morison, Samuel Eliot
The Rising Sun in the Pacific, 1931–April 1942 (History of United States Naval Operations in World War II, Vol. III). Boston: Little, Brown and Company, 1948.

Pratt, Fletcher
The Marines' War. New York: Wm. Sloane Associates, Inc., 1948.

Index

142

About the Author

Irving Werstein has made writing both his goal and his life. Even when he was officially a factory worker, a salesman, or an actor and comedian, Mr. Werstein spent his free moments writing.

He served in the U. S. Army from 1941 to 1945 and was a correspondent for *Yank* magazine. After the war he devoted all his time to writing; he has written magazine stories, radio and television scripts, and a number of books.

Mr. Werstein was born in Brooklyn, New York, and has lived in Mexico, Italy, and England. He has traveled extensively in Holland, Denmark, and France. He lives in Stuyvesant Town in New York City with his wife and young son.